Blessing
to you [...]
and your [...]

Mike & Martha
Cahoon

MW00768963

LIVING WITH A SPORTSMAN
AND OTHER WILD THINGS

*A Daily Devotional to Inspire Laughter
and Fellowship with the Creator of Joy*

Martha McCoy Cahoon

WESTBOW
PRESS®
A DIVISION OF THOMAS NELSON
& ZONDERVAN

Copyright © 2017 Martha McCoy Cahoon.

All rights reserved. No part of this book may be used or reproduced by any means, graphic, electronic, or mechanical, including photocopying, recording, taping or by any information storage retrieval system without the written permission of the author except in the case of brief quotations embodied in critical articles and reviews.

This book is a work of non-fiction. Unless otherwise noted, the author and the publisher make no explicit guarantees as to the accuracy of the information contained in this book and in some cases, names of people and places have been altered to protect their privacy.

New American standard, 1978 The Ryrie, Charles Caldwell. 1960, 1962, 1963, 1968, 1971,1972,1973,1975,1977,1995 by The Lockman Foundation. Used by permission all rights reserved.

Scriptures quotations marked "TLB" are taken from The Living Bible/ KIenneth N. Taylor. Tyndale House, Copyright 1997, 1971 by Tyndale House Publishers, Inc. Used by permission. All rights reserved.

Scripture quotations marked "Msg" are taken from The Message, copyright 1993,1994, 1995, 1996, 2000,, 2001,2002. Used by permission of Nav Press Publishing Group.

Requests for information should be addressed to:
Living With a Sportsman and Other Wild Things
marthamccoon@gmail.com

WestBow Press books may be ordered through booksellers or by contacting:

WestBow Press
A Division of Thomas Nelson & Zondervan
1663 Liberty Drive
Bloomington, IN 47403
www.westbowpress.com
1 (866) 928-1240

Because of the dynamic nature of the Internet, any web addresses or links contained in this book may have changed since publication and may no longer be valid. The views expressed in this work are solely those of the author and do not necessarily reflect the views of the publisher, and the publisher hereby disclaims any responsibility for them.

Any people depicted in stock imagery provided by Thinkstock are models, and such images are being used for illustrative purposes only.
Certain stock imagery © Thinkstock.

ISBN: 978-1-5127-8927-0 (sc)
ISBN: 978-1-5127-8929-4 (hc)
ISBN: 978-1-5127-8928-7 (e)

Library of Congress Control Number: 2017909618

Print information available on the last page.

WestBow Press rev. date: 07/03/2017

DEDICATION

I dedicate this book to my older brother, Roger
McCoy, and his wife, Delores, who loved me enough
to safeguard my life spiritually and directionally.

I also dedicate this book to parents and
grandparents who came before us and lived lives
of good courage and Christ like example.

CONTENTS

Back of the Woodshed

INTRODUCTION

On a brisk autumn morning I was driving up Highway 35 headed toward north Alabama on a speaking engagement. In the sparse traffic I eased my car in behind a pick-up truck with three men in the cab. Despite my distance from them, it was obvious to me they were having a good time.

Each man was wearing a baseball cap and a tuff of hair was sticking out of the hole in the back of the cap. The men were likely on their way to work and had stopped at a fast food restaurant for breakfast because each had a steaming cup of coffee and a biscuit in his hands.

The men could have been from any walk in life I supposed, from a physicist at the near-by missile site to a clerk at the local feed and seed store. However, their station in life did not matter; they were simply enjoying each other's company and having a good ole time on their drive to work. I imagined they were telling comical stories about their lives, past and present, and enjoying the full comedy of it all.

As I continued to follow closely behind the trio, the thought crossed my mind, "I wonder what it would take for these men to read something of a spiritual nature before they leave their homes in the mornings?" Suddenly, the voice within me spoke, "Something with humor."

I rolled the thought over in my mind… something with humor…that would also be spiritual? "How do you do that Lord?" I asked.

"You, Martha, write a devotion book and tell these men the funny, crazy stories that Mike has told about himself and his friends while they were hunting, fishing and living life. Then add a few comical stories about your own Lucille Ball experiences as a wife and mother for their wives to enjoy as well."

"And you can teach them something spiritual in that Lord?" …I asked in my spiritual conversation.

"Everybody likes to laugh Martha, particularly when they can identify with you and may have experienced the same life story. Then while you have their attention…tell them a story about who I Am from My Book that I wrote, as well."

"But you know Father, I failed English 101 in college and I had to take the class again. How can I write a devotion book? My writing and grammar skills sound a lot like my spoken verbiage…back porch Southern!"

"I know…I was there when you failed the class and when we passed it the second time…which is why I wrote Luke 1:37 years ago, 'For nothing will be impossible with God.' Just go to work Martha."

THINGS THAT FLY, THINGS THAT CRAWL, THINGS THAT SWIM

Hunter's Rap

No time to go huntin',
Now that's a crying shame.
No time to go huntin',
Now who are you going to blame?

You make time to go huntin'
No need for rhyme or reason.
Make time to go huntin'
Your excuse is, "It's in season!"

FISH DOG

It was the first day of March and quail season was over. There would be an end to bird talk, bird dogs and birds shot, much to my husband, Mike's regret. Mike is a hunter. In fact, he was born 200 years too late because his real name is Daniel Boone Cahoon and no one bothered to tell me that when I married him. He loves to hunt most anything that moves in the woods, but especially he loves to quail hunt.

Quail hunting encompasses everything that he enjoys as a hunter --- the feel of a fine gun and the responsibility of knowing how and when it should be used, the practiced skill of a marksman hitting a quail in flight and later savoring the taste of this delicacy with biscuit and brown gravy. And Mike's favorite part, the rewarding experience of working with well-trained dogs. Of course, all of this is enjoyed while surrounded by nature in all of its grandeur. An added bonus to push him over the top of the scale of hunter's ecstasy is to have a hunting buddy experience all of this with him. No man could ask for more, and according to Mike, this is as good as it gets.

We had been out of college only a few years and were saving for the great American dream, a home of our own. But at the time we lived at the end of a gravel road in a rented house in a rural area in Athens, Georgia. The house was comfortable, but to make our living conditions more inviting, our landlord had offered to pay for any improvements that we made to the property.

An area that desperately needed muscle and creativity was the landscaping. The creativity came easily because I had long pictured blooming rhododendrons and azaleas planted in just the right places. And of course the great hunter would now have the time to provide the muscle that I needed to get this work accomplished.

Now...I knew convincing Mike to provide the muscle would take some coaxing on my part. To be honest, I knew it would take more than coaxing; it would take a half nelson wrestling hold and homemade biscuits for breakfast for a month to persuade Mike that the work needed to be done. Not only would he need coaxing but he would need re-educating as well. After leaving work at 5:00pm each day this intelligent man discarded American English and spoke only "bubbabonics" which meant the word "landscaping" was not in his vocabulary. Mike's idea of landscaping was rolling any old tires laying around the yard to the back of the house or taking his recliner off the front porch and tying his bird dogs to a shade tree for weed control (rotating the dogs to a new tree weekly of course). His appreciation of yard space narrowed down to one word... functional. In his opinion a functional yard meant having enough room to park a pick up truck and train a bird dog. If those requirements were satisfied---he was happy.

The house was on a lake that was well- stocked with large bass and pan-sized brim. Our friends who fished there said it was a fisherman's paradise. However, the lake was no threat to my sports-loving husband's time because he had never fished or even had any desire to learn. He preferred a rifle to a reel any day.

On this beautiful March morning, Mike and I and a bird dog named Kate, strolled along the mossy banks of the lake at the back of the house. The spring air and the freshness of the day felt good as we breathed deeply. The lake was spring-fed and we stopped and stood on an inlet near the mouth of one of the springs. The water there was shallow and filled with silt and lake grasses. We noticed a slight ripple in the water and to our surprise saw a large-mouth bass lying lazily at the water's edge. Apparently it had chased a school of small fish into this shallow area and was enjoying an easy meal.

An old Zebco reel, abandoned by one of the children months earlier, was lying on the bank. Mike picked up the rusty old reel with its rotten line and plastic worm and cast in the direction of the fish. Despite his unpracticed casting, the worm fell a few inches from the fish.

The lazy bass and plastic worm lay side by side in the shallow water long enough for me to be thankful Mike knew nothing about fishing and that my new azaleas and rhododendrons would have his undivided attention the remainder of the spring and summer.

Suddenly, the fish lunged for the worm and barely hung the hook in its mouth. Mike, in a startled spasm, jerked the reel hard to set the hook and hollered in surprise, (using Bubbabonics) "Well looka here, he took it!"

In his inexperience, Mike did not know that when a bass is hooked it will either surge to deep water or jump. With the water being shallow, it had to jump and it did about five times. During this time, Mike looked like a clown in a rodeo as he hopped, staggered and stumbled around on the bank with the question written all over his face, "What do I do next?"

Finally, the fish made one last effort at a mighty jump and landed near the bank on the opposite side of the inlet in less than six inches of water. Stunned, the bass rolled over on its side and the hook fell out of its mouth. There it lay...exhausted and free.

Without a second thought, Mike, using very poor form, did a standing broad jump into the cold, calf-deep water. He gave a startled gasp and his eyes bugged out as big as saucers from the shock of the cold---but they stayed riveted on the fish. In one swift motion, he scooped the fish up with his hands and threw it in the direction of the bank. The fish, flying through the air, bounced off of Kate the bird dog that was standing on the bank. Kate, adding to the bizarre gymnastics, did a startled flip and landed on the fish. I stood in amazement watching this carnival of events and knew that if I had not seen it I would not have believed it. Kate, who was as amazed as I, was accustomed to pointing birds that flew from the ground into the sky, but she was not sure what to do with fish that fell out of the sky onto the ground. But instinct took over and she did what came natural, she pointed the fish.

The nine-pound bass was mounted and hung on a wall in the den of our rented home a few weeks later. Several other fine trophies were caught and mounted that summer as well, but they were caught without the help of Kate the bird dog. Needless to say, there were no azaleas and rhododendrons blooming in my yard that year.

**"*Wherefore, accept one another, just as Christ also
accept us to the glory of God.*" Romans 15:7**

I have often thought it would be interesting to create a video game
involving two characters who are opposites in personality. The
two individuals would be placed in a controlled environment,
given an assignment to be completed together and their
individual scores kept with points added or subtracted as they
attempt to succeed in their work. I have even gone so far as
to imagine the character of each personality and what their
assignments would be.

One individual would be an A type personality who is a
visionary, self motivated, goal-focused individual who locks
onto his or her goal like a missile and moves forward until the
objective is accomplished. In this electronic game I see this
character played by a rhino.

The second individual would be a melancholy personality
who goes through life a dreamer, is a perfectionist, thrives on
interaction with people and his or her work production depends
upon his mood at the time. In the electronic game I see this
character played by a peacock.

The assignment to be completed by the rhino and peacock
working together can be one of a number of scenarios depending
upon the level of stress the game player chooses to play. But for
the sake of example let us set up a game and have our two
characters repair a broken dam before floodwaters engulf
them. The proposed game plans seem reasonable enough, but
let us watch the two solve the emerging problem in order to
save themselves and a small fictitious community that is being
threatened downstream below the dam.

The rhino rises to the occasion first...of course. True to his or her personality traits this character quickly assesses the situation around him, then lowers his nose and charges forward with exploding power. He spouts orders to everyone within hearing distance and those not paying attention he mows down as he follows the straightest path between himself and his sighted goal. Too bad he never looks behind him to notice the wounded bodies, trampled feelings and bleeding egos he left in his wake. Nevertheless, his work performance leads to productivity and he makes great strides toward repairing the dam.

But where is our other character in this game? True to personality, the peacock eventually arrives, says hello to each person on site then walks carefully onto the alarming scene and abruptly stops. He slowly spreads his beautiful tail feathers, holds his head high, picks one foot up carefully, pauses, and contemplates quietly. Then he unexpectedly changes directions, does a circled pirouette and rushes off in a calculated direction to work on the problem. Of course everyone on the scene is chest deep in water because peacock took so much time in the preparation details he almost arrived too late to be of any help.

Would this be a challenging dollar's worth of entertainment or what? Imagine the adrenalin rush the player at the controls would experience as he tries to get these two personalities to work together as they struggle against rising water, the clock and a variety of obstacles, not to mention their personality differences.

But look around you! We see this game being played out everyday and guess what? We are the players! Life is made up of relationship trials in every area of our lives and most particularly in the marriage.

Does this game reveal to us that we should discourage marriages between peacock and rhino personalities? Not necessarily. Opposites attracting opposites can make a wonderful marriage. And even the best union of similarities in personalities and temperaments in a man and woman will not guarantee a happy, compatible relationship unless God is in the middle of the marriage.

God made each man and woman unique---no two people are completely identical. He gave us personality strengths to be used in our lives to glorify Him and personality weaknesses to glorify Him as well. Careful, we are now talking about real life people; we are no longer playing a video game. So how does one glorify God in their weakness? We do so by allowing God to change those weaknesses into His likeness so that our weaknesses become God's strengths lived through us. II Corinthians 5:17 says, "Therefore if any man is in Christ, he is a new creature; the old things passed away; behold, new things have come."

So how does this fit into the rhino and peacock relationship? The Bible says, "Wherefore, accept one another, just as Christ also accepted us to the glory of God." (Romans 15:7) No doubt, each marriage partner has personality quirks that can drive their spouse up the wall. But despite these quirks we are to accept each other (warts and all) and love unconditionally as Christ loves and accepts us unconditionally. In doing this, God teaches us a greater capacity for acceptance and love, which we may not learn otherwise.

Does this mean that the weak and hurting traits exhibited by a marriage partner go unchecked forever while continuing to make excuses like, "It's not my fault that I am this way, my parents were this way and it's their fault" or "This is just who I am." No, according to God's Word we are each responsible for our own actions and sins. But the good news is---where we are weak God is strong. But in order for us to draw upon His strength we must first know and accept His Son, Jesus Christ, as our savior and live with a growing knowledge of His Word. You can use your background as an excuse for present bad behavior only until you receive Jesus Christ as your personal Lord and Savior. After that we have a new power, the Holy Spirit, within us that will give us the strength and direction we need to change our conduct.

Hopefully at this point all Rhinos and Peacocks serious about working on their relationships in the marriage may ask, "Is there a program to follow?" Sure there is a program, it is found in Galatians 5:22 and 23, "But the fruit of the Spirit is love, joy, peace, patience, kindness, goodness, faithfulness, gentleness, self-control; against such things there is no law." Developing these positive qualities into our personality by the power of the Holy Spirit is a sure way to strengthen our Christian lives and our marriages as well.

Also, these fruit of the Spirit will build our natural strengths even stronger and at the same time develop our weaknesses into strengths while we still maintain our own INDIVIDUALITY! God never created us as robots. So if He created an individual with a Rhino-like personality, they will remain a Rhino, just a gentler more sensitive, Christ like Rhino. If He created an individual with a Peacock like personality, they will remain a Peacock, just a more responsible, alert and Christ like peacock. Remember, each person is created unique and God does not want to change our uniqueness because that enables us to do the work He has planned for us to do here on earth.

Paul explained this in 2 Timothy 3:16-17 (Living Bible) so well, "The whole Bible was given to us by inspiration from God and is useful to teach us what is true and to make us realize what is wrong in our lives; it straightens us out and helps us do what is right. Verse 17: It is God's way of making us well prepared at every point, fully equipped to do good to everyone.

The truth in this verse makes it hard for us to go wrong and easy to go right…if we are willing to steadily press into it.

DAY 2

RUBBERNECK CARP

We had finally bought our first house and it was brand new. At last I was within the boundaries of civilization. Because Mike's hobbies included hunting and fishing, we had always lived in houses in isolated areas where bird dogs could be kept and trained. And of course if there was a lake nearby for fishing that made heaven on earth as far as Mike was concerned.

We had been married ten years before I learned a concrete driveway was an option for house dwellers. We usually lived on a dirt road in the middle of nowhere, without neighbors, in houses at least 50 years old and usually in need of repair. Mike saw all of this as great southern living, but for a man who was barely housetrained so it was hard to appreciate his taste.

Finally we were in a new subdivision with acres of concrete and manicured lawns. It was wonderful as far as I was concerned. There was no red Georgia clay to track into the house, no giant field rats coming in for the winter, and the bird dogs seemed to have adjusted to a nice pen in the back of the house.

In fact, everyone had adjusted to this move beautifully. The children had other children to play with rather than just our cats and dogs. Even Mike was making the transition well. Of course the new bass boat in the garage helped a lot.

Mike was learning how to become a good fisherman. This new sport opened up a whole new world for him, not that hunting everything that moved in the woods was not enough thrill to satisfy him. Not only did he love to catch the fish but we loved to eat them as well. Fried fish with hushpuppies and cold slaw is great southern cuisine. And we enjoyed most every fish that Mike pulled from the Georgian lakes, except for carp. Mike said that carp was a trash fish, so he threw them back. However, since our move, there was no lake near the house, so many days he would go into our front yard to work on his casting skills. He was a perfectionist at things important to him so he spent many hours practicing his technique with the reel. But rather than using a fishing plug with hooks, he used a heavy rubber plug designed for practice.

One Sunday afternoon, he decided that he would go into the front yard to practice. On his last fishing trip, using his new reel, he had thrown 500 times and backlashed 500 times. In a subdivision Sunday afternoon is usually the time when house hunters drive around looking for houses for sale. The houses on either side of us were for sale (perhaps the bird dogs needed more adjustment that I thought) so there was quite a parade of prospective buyers driving by all afternoon. Mike, non too complimentary, called these drivers, "rubberneckers," obviously because they turned their heads from side to side as they drove down a street, stretching to look at houses on each side of the street. They drove by slowly, time after time, getting a good look at the houses and one car in particular passed by several times.

During this time Mike continued to cast his line refining his technique. He was becoming pretty aggravated with all the traffic, the engine noise and fuel exhaust. At the moment, if he had his choice of dust from a dirt road or carbon monoxide from an exhaust pipe, the latter would lose…no doubt.

Finally the one very curious car passed by again and slowed to a rolling stop as it neared our lawn. A man grinning from ear to ear rolled down his window and yelled, "Are you catching anything?" Mike, most irritated at this invasion of privacy slowly reeled in the line, pulled the bill of his cap down farther over his face and answered, "Yeah, just hung a rubberneck carp." The intruding driver suddenly decided the chances of a good neighbor were slim on this street so he decided to look elsewhere…and he did, in a hurry.

Conduct yourself with wisdom toward outsiders, making the most of the opportunity. Let your speech always be with grace, seasoned, as it were, with salt, so that you may know how you should respond to each person. **Colossians 4:5 & 6**

Someone once said, "If you have an unpleasant neighbor, the odds are that he does too." Too often people bring out the worst in each other, particularly when privacy and boundary issues come into the picture. Human nature has a tendency to build fences around their territory and only allows close family and the select persons that they enjoy or feel comfortable with inside their fence of relationships.

In our busy culture there is little time or desire to deal with outsiders and uninvited intruders. This is especially the attitude while shopping, working, driving a car and generally mingling with society. Space violation is a real source of irritation.

I do not believe that this is the way that God desires for us to manage our lives. I wonder if occasionally He maneuvers outsiders into our space for a purpose. This is why it is most important for Christians to check their mouths, facial expressions and attitudes when they "accidentally" bump into that person outside their select space zone. This could be a divine appointment and clamping our jaws and pinching all the muscles in our face like we are in the middle of a root canal is not the way to diplomacy.

Missionary, Chuck Quinley, in his book, "I Want to Bear Fruit!" challenges readers to pray a prayer each morning. The prayer says simply, "Lord, send me someone today who needs your help." He goes on to say, "There are millions of sincere, searching people out there. Their sighs come up to God as prayers begging Him to send someone to tell them how to find peace. God will answer their prayers with you. He will arrange coincidences to seat you together or to connect you in conversation. He will give you the words and the power to speak for Him, but we have to present ourselves to Him as workers who show up for work."

Is this a jolting concept or what? With this thought in mind obviously it is important that we *speak in wisdom seasoned with salt* when God opens the door for an opportunity to speak to someone. If we Believers are the salt of the earth, then we should be able to speak tasty seasonings into the meat of conversation when God sends someone in need of His direction.

Be sensitive and make the most of the opportunity with that person who may sit down beside you at the dentist office or one who cuts in line in front of you at the grocery store. The old habit of overly protecting your space rights may be a habit that God wants you to break. Understand that habits are like cork or lead, they tend to keep you up or hold you down. Salt can never be held down, it penetrates, preserves and purifies.

Salt also seasons and its presence is welcomed, because when used in correct amounts it whets the taste buds to want more. So maybe we should check how people react toward us as they near our space zone. Is our presence savored or severed?

In wisdom---make the most of the opportunity.

DAY 3

REPTILE REAL ESTATE

It was the last day of quail season and Mike and his friend, Durkee, had been invited to go hunting on a farm near Albany, Georgia in Lee County. The temperature was more that 70 degrees and had been for several days and too hot to go quail hunting. But when a man has a chance to go to prime quail territory, he has to go.

They had their best two dogs with them, Kate, a white setter, ticked with lemon. And there was the notorious Tater Bug, a liver pointer heavily ticked and ugly except when hunting. Both men agreed that these dogs were so smart they could run across a man's farm and later tell him how many coveys of quail he had on the farm when they loaded back up in the truck. They were that good.

Since the weather was so warm the farm manager for the property warned them strongly to stay off the ridges. Mike thought that was strange because a man could stand anywhere and see a hundred miles or just about. But a ridge to a south Georgian flatlander is a three to six-inch elevation, or according to Mike a slope to none a tall'.

However, the problem with the ridges is that gofer turtles dig holes in them for a place to live and rattlesnakes will also occupy the same hole during cold weather. But in 70 degree temperatures the rattlesnakes will begin to crawl out, seeking the warm spring sun. Mike and Durkee acknowledged the warning and left to hunt.

The two men were enjoying the day of hunting and working their dogs when Mike suddenly found himself on a ridge and began to see gofer holes. Durkee was off to the side of Mike several yards on lower ground. Mike was cautiously watching for holes as he was hunting when suddenly he saw a snake's tail with a dozen rattles on the end of it.

According to Mike's story, he froze instinctively and never made a sound. According to Durkee, Mike jumped three feet in the air and bellowed like a bull, which is a Georgian's way of saying, "I'm scared slap to death!" In either case, Mike began looking wildly for the snake's head and after what seemed like an enormous distance from the tail---he saw it! The blunt head was about the size of Mike's fist and it was rapidly moving into striking position with the rattles on the tail in full serenade.

In a protective reaction, Mike shouldered his 20 gauge shotgun and lowered the over populated snake inhabitants by one. Then he pivoted to run in the opposite direction and ran head-on into Durkee. As much as Mike would have liked to look like a brave character in a Louis L'Amour western, he did not. He more closely resembled Goofy in the comic strips.

"How big is it?" asked Durkee after they bounced off each other. "If it had legs it could have been an alligator," answered Mike. Durkee took one look at the snake, turned and looked Mike straight in the eyes and said, "Brother, quail season is over, I'm going to the truck." Mike followed with no hesitation.

> **"Be on alert, stand firm in the faith, act like**
> **men, be strong." I Corinthians 16:13**

A hundred years added to man's history has done him no favors in regard to assurance of his and his family's safety. In contrast, a hundred years ago the enemy was clearly defined. Man instantly recognized a wicked treasure-seeking pirate, a deadly wild panther, a wild, stampeding herd of buffalo or a nest of slithering rattlesnakes, and he avoided them at all cost.

Today the enemy is much more cleverly disguised. He hides under the cloak of the 21st century, dressed handsomely in the smooth talk of compromise, selfish ambition and individual rights. Often it is difficult to recognize him and the potential threat he makes upon our lives, but nevertheless, he is present with an agenda all his own.

If we examined this enemy with God's wisdom we would see him as subtle disregard for family values by permitting the sanctity of marriage to be redefined. Or he may appear as an opportunity for a quick and easy financial success with a "small" compromise of character. He delights in convincing us that it is okay that modern culture places no boundaries on morals and purity. He may tell us the principles that our country was founded upon are antiquated and out of date and that God and country are the impossible dream. None of these voices bare angry fangs or scream out blood-chilling howls but they are our enemies and the threat upon our lives is just as deadly.

For a man to conquer this enemy and live a quality of life today and in the future he must be on the alert and well- informed about current events and the decisions that society is making around him. He must have a high moral sense of right and wrong and be willing to stand firm on Godly convictions. He must know without doubt that the modern enemy is shrewd and without conscience, setting traps for those that are complacent or "too busy to be bothered." So how can man see through the disguises and clearly appraise the truth?

God's word is the true standard to test the world around us. The scriptures tell us that God will bring to light the things hidden in the darkness and disclose the motives of men's hearts (see I Corinthians 4:5). For this reason it is important for men to read God's Word before considering business opportunities or forming opinions in regard to our country's political direction. Understanding God's Word is important as a father follows his child's progress in the school's curriculum. It is important as he and his family sit down to view television at night; he must discern, is this program entertainment or moral injury?

As a man gathers his facts from the world, he must *fortify* his understanding by daily applying God's Word. Nahum 2:1 (Living Bible) says it so well, "...You are already surrounded by enemy armies! Sound the alarm! Man the ramparts! Muster your defenses, full force, and keep a sharp watch for the enemy attack to begin!" This certainly sounds like a battle cry, spurring men onward to many degrees of heroism. But before one can be a hero he must "act like a man." Let's apply our scripture in I Corinthians 16:13 to our lives, "Be on alert, stand firm in the faith, act like men, be strong." I believe it will not only give men the strength to "act like a man" but to act like men of God.

DAY 4

COLUMN KILLER

A family is blessed to have one or more friends who have a great sense of humor and loves to laugh. Just being in their presence is a delight. Mike and I have several of these type friends but one in particular, Jerry, has given much joy to our family.

Jerry has a Will Rogers type of thought-provoking humor that catches you unexpectedly and leaves you laughing for hours. He had an engineering degree from Georgia Tech, but strangely enough, he had a reputation for repairing everything in his path with rope and duck tape. At this particular time he drove a gray Ford pick-up truck that he had driven for years and it looked as if Fred Sanford used it for his junkyard chores. He had no fewer than twenty-five bumper stickers on the rear bumper so tailgaters had a great literary workout when they were behind him in traffic.

Jerry drove his vintage vehicle to our home on a dark Saturday morning at five o'clock to join Mike on a trip to the woods going turkey hunting. At the driveway entrance to our home there were two large six-foot columns that I had paid a brick mason to build just a few weeks earlier. These columns had been a vision of mine when we had built the house and I had pinched pennies in the family budget and used some resourceful ideas to earn the money to pay for them. To say I was pleased with the columns was an understatement, I was proud to the bone about them.

Later in the morning after Mike and Jerry had been in the woods for several hours, I decided to go into town to take care of some errands. As I drove out of our drive and neared our entrance, there to my horror, lay one of my beautiful columns on its side. I could not believe my eyes! Like a fallen sentry that had been ambushed, it lay in the red Georgia clay with a vacant hole in the ground where it once stood. It should have taken a bulldozer to push it over it was so heavy.

I jumped from my car to examine the damage and found the bricks were chipped on one corner with gray paint encrusted in the area. I turned my head in a sweeping surveillance of the yard and my eyes instantly settled on Jerry's truck sitting innocently in our drive. I quickly stomped over to the truck to look for incriminating evidence. A close examination revealed red brick marks on the rear bumper by a sticker that read, "I'm so old I don't buy green bananas." At once I had a mental picture of Jerry's driving habits and remembered he always backed up at fifty miles an hour and obviously my brick column had gotten in the way that dark morning.

I knew the men would be in from hunting at anytime and even though I was sure the column could be repaired, I was not going to let Jerry get away with this stunt without speaking my mind. So before leaving I wrote a note and taped it on our front door that read, "Jerry, if you think I did not notice... I did!"... Martha. I could have said more...a lot more. But I felt a few well-chosen words reflected my superb mental capacity and emotional control. So I left it at that.

Around noon I returned home and drove into my driveway passing by my wounded column lying on its side. The men had returned from hunting as well and Jerry and his demolition truck were gone. As I reached the front door, I glanced at my note that I had left earlier for Jerry and below my message he had scribbled, "Notice what?" ...Jerry.

I wished I had said more...a lot more. Now it was too late, the moment lost, and to make matters worse I was sure Jerry was on his way home to get a new supply of rope and duck tape to repair my fallen column.

> *"And be kind to one another, tenderhearted,*
> *forgiving each other, just as God in Christ*
> *also has forgiven you." Ephesians 4:32*

The difference between a deep and lasting friendship and a broken friendship that is swept aside can be found in the word forgiveness. Any relationship that desires to grow deeply will be tested by personal crisis, differing opinions and conflicting personalities that may result in hurt feelings and misunderstandings. Unless the parties involved apply forgiveness, a worn bed sheet will eventually measure the depth of the relationship.

It is interesting that in the same sentence of this scripture in Ephesians the two words, *kind* and *tenderhearted*, are mentioned with the word *forgiveness*. Perhaps the reason for this is that these two actions are necessary, or will work hand in hand, with true forgiveness. It is next to impossible to forgive someone completely and Christ-like if we remain angry, bitter and hardhearted.

In the area of forgiveness Christ is the ultimate teacher and example. His death upon the cross made the supreme sacrifice so that all humanity could be forgiven; and not only did Christ give his life for us, but our attention should examine the example of His life as He gave it for us. In many ways our reactions are very different from His.

- He gave Himself willingly...not while kicking and screaming reply, "I will not!"
- He gave Himself completely...not with a defiant shrug answer, "I'll forgive, but not forget!"
- He gave Himself unconditionally... not with a pointed finger retort, "I'll go this far, but I was hurt too badly to go any farther!"
- He gave Himself sacrificially, never replying, "I'm not willing to pay the price!"

Using Jesus' example of love, sacrifice and forgiveness is the action we should apply in regard to relationships. Very few of us will be asked to give our lives for the sake of a friendship, but for many people, the act of dying looks far more inviting than asking or granting forgiveness.

Do we choose to be stiff-necked with our backs turned from forgiveness rather than being kind and tenderhearted with our hearts breaking with forgiveness? Life is richer because God blesses us sweetly through the gift of friendship. Someone said it so well when they said, "Friendship doubles our joy and divides our grief." It is hard to believe this precious gift can be jeopardized because we are not willing to say four words, "Will you forgive me?" or "Yes, I forgive you."

GOTTA' BITE!

Hippocrates once said, "Let what you eat become your medicine and your medicine what you eat." If this is true, Mike and his friend, Jerry, are two men who have overdosed quite a number of times on their medication.

Their appetites are quite enormous and delicate words such as "bon appétit" are completely wasted and should be replaced with "pig out" and "chow down".

One of the few things they had rather do than eat is fish and if they can do both at the same time they are in hog heaven. In fact, they have done both at the same time on a number of occasions.

Their method of operation is simple. They decide on a lake that seems right, which depends on the season, temperature and the mood they are in at the time. Then they pack their favorite lunch, which consists of cold drinks, peanut butter crackers and Jerry's favorite, a Vidalia onion sandwich and if he has it a slice of roast beef. Then they are off for the day.

It was just such a day that they had decided to go fishing in a night tournament at Lake Lanier near Gainesville, Georgia. The tournament started at six o'clock in the evening and ended at one o'clock in the morning.

The most exciting part of these tournaments is the takeoff at the opening of the event. The boats rev their engines straining for the explosion of power and the air is filled with smoke and water spray. The noise is deafening and the men love it.

The two men decided to use Mike's Allison Craft bass boat which had a 150 horsepower motor and ran about 65 miles an hour. Time is most important, so when the signal is given for the tournament to begin, each boat speeds away with exploding power to a promising spot.

The starting signal was finally given and Mike and Jerry raced across the water. Both had their "I'm having more fun than I can stand" grins on and their eyes squinted against the water spray and sun. To avoid losing valuable fishing time eating supper, Jerry decided to test one of his Vidalia sandwiches while they were en route to a spot they had scouted out earlier in the week.

Mike was driving the boat and did not realize that Jerry had a hunger attack. They were moving across the water at about 60 miles an hour and the front of the boat was sitting up so high that practically the only thing in the water was the prop.

Eventually, Mike glanced over his shoulder in Jerry's direction just in time to see the fight of the evening.

Jerry was holding his sandwich in both hands and was preparing to take a bite. But the wind from the speeding boat was so strong that the two slices of bread were separating and flapping wildly, leaving the onion naked and exposed in the late evening sun.

Mike almost lost control of the boat as he watched Jerry's mouth wide open and taste buds salivating as he tried to trap the bread around the onion with his lips so he could chomp down.

Mike could have been a gentleman and slowed the boat so a friend could enjoy his supper…but no! The catch in the rear of the boat might be the most challenging fight he saw all night. And of course, Mike had a reputation for having no mercy when an opportunity for a good belly laugh was in sight.

The wind blew hard and at the moment it looked as if Jerry would win, experience had the better hand. His primate-looking lips were curled around the slices of bread and his tongue was salivating Then, suddenly control changed! Jerry's hat blew off and he instinctively used one hand to grab for it. With only one hand on the sandwich the bread was again loose, slapping him about the face and across the nose. Control was slipping away and he seemed helpless to reverse it. Could it be this food connoisseur was staring defeat in the mouth? No! Not for this veteran chowhound. With all the skill and talent of a professional, Jerry wrestled the sandwich under his grip and with straining lips he at last experienced the taste of victory.

Finally, Mike slowly trimmed the boat and pulled into a promising fishing spot as his friend, with both jaws bulging; put the finishing touches to his catch.

"Follow me and I will make you fishers of men."
Matthew 4:19

Peter was a fisherman. He fished with all the zeal and strength that he could heave from his body. All his life he had thrown himself into his work and he was most likely an A type personality. If Peter had been asked what his drive in life was, he may possibly have said, "To fish for fish."

Then Jesus entered Peter's life. Peter saw in Jesus a man much like himself in drive and determination but with a message and method that seemed impossible for a man of Peter's design to understand.

Jesus asked Peter to follow him and Peter, never dreaming he would, did, and began a most extraordinary journey that completely changed his life.

On this journey, Peter developed a personal relationship with Jesus and became completely absorbed in the person of Jesus Christ. In developing this relationship, Peter found zeal in life that he had never experienced, a joy in life he had not celebrated and a strength in life that was beyond his own.

Prior to this relationship, he had been a fisherman who happened to know about God. Now, he was a follower of Christ who happened to be a fisherman.

Later in the scripture, Jesus asked His disciples, "But who do you say I am?" Peter was the first to answer, "Thou art the Christ, the Son of the living God." This journey with Jesus had equipped Peter with a depth finder enabling him to see deeper spiritually than other men and allowing Jesus to make Peter a fisher of men.

In the book of Acts, Peter continues to exhibit great energy and zeal for his work. But after his experience with Jesus, I believe that if he had been asked what motivated his drive in life, his response would have been, "To fish for men!"

A personal relationship with Jesus results in this attitude...the desire to go fishing.

DAY 6

DOUBLE JEOPARDY

Rattlesnake season in South Georgia is a thing taken seriously by the residing population. They know from experience that it is wise to follow every precaution and take as few risks as possible during this precarious time of the year. In fact, several counties have a "Rattlesnake Round-up" to help control the snake population.

It was during rattlesnake season in Greenbush, Georgia, a town south of Albany, that Mike's friend, David, was planting pine trees. This was a job that needed to be done, even at this risky time of the year, so he was on guard constantly in case he encountered one of these music-making reptiles.

Because of recent rains, the soil was too wet for a tractor, so David was planting with a diplor. Mike says a diplor is a gizmo used by a person with a strong back and a weak mind. Mike also admits that he has quite a few gizmos himself. Technically, a diplor is a three foot long T-shaped iron spike used to push a hole into the ground large enough to plant a pine seedling.

David was making fair progress with the work and had just made a hole with the diplor and was bending over, placing a pine seedling into the ground. Suddenly, through the weeds, he saw the head of a rattlesnake, not six inches from his hand.

The rattler saw him at about the same time and instantly began to move into attack position.

When unexpected, dangerous situations like this arise, a man does not usually sit down and plan his next step in coping with the problem, or at least David did not. Self-preservation set in and panic took over.

Instinctively he swung at the snake with his diplor and jumped backwards. With all of his senses at maximum charge, David stood poised to strike again. He knew his blow had connected but was not sure if it had been fatal. His eyes and head were jerking from right to left like a runaway windshield wiper, straining to see if he had finished the snake.

Suddenly he was aware of something brushing his right leg. He wasn't sure what it was but the sensation was unnerving to say the least. He looked down and realized when he had jumped backwards in striking the first snake he landed on a second rattlesnake and had pinned it to the ground with his left foot about six inches from its head. The snake was angrily striking at David's right leg, which was just barely out of biting range.

If there were an Olympic event for high backwards jumping, David would have a gold medal on his coffee table today. When he jumped back this time, he swung wildly with the diplor and connected a fatal blow on the second snake's head. Frantically he checked the area for the first snake and much to his relief found it dead also.

With weak knees, he managed to walk to his pick-up truck a few yards away. He sat down on the tailgate and removed his boots and pulled his pants legs up to see if he had been bitten by the second snake he'd been standing on. His heart was racing so fast he was afraid of a heart attack and he wanted to know in case he died, if it was from snake bite, heart trauma or both. Fortunately, he suffered neither.

A convenience store on Highway 19 paid $1.50 a foot for live Rattlesnakes and $1.00 a foot for dead Rattlesnakes. David collected $9.00 from the store that day after he finished planting pine trees.

> *"Or if he shall ask for a fish, he will not give*
> *him a snake, will he? Matthew 7:10*

Many Christians, when in hard places in life, have a habit of singing a country western song entitled, "Achy Breaky Heart." Their hearts are breaking over hurtful circumstances in their lives and they are wondering where the satisfying life is that God promises.

We cry out, "Lord, I want to have a glorifying testimony for you but painful circumstances continue to come into my life that distract and slow me down in my spiritual walk." We take on long, pouty faces and as a result the world cannot see the testimony for the tears, even though God can certainly shine through our tears. But unfortunately, we often allow the tears to turn into whining, whimpering and wailing and God must get very disappointed in us.

God's people often forget that the most powerful testimony His children can give Him in the midst of hurting times and hard places is praise. God tells us to give Him a sacrifice of praise during these times even though we don't feel like praising Him. (Hebrews 13:15) Not only is this an opportunity for a glorifying testimony to God, but it is an opportunity to grow deeper in the spiritual truths that God desires to teach us. No saint ever received a higher degree of faith and spiritual insights by sitting safely in a kindergarten sandbox. A higher degree in faith may require walking through what looks like a snake pit at the time. And most likely if we have the courage to take the walk, we are asking, "Lord, you are not going to give me a snake…are you?"

The snake pit represents the trials, tribulations, or hard places in life that require walking step by step in faith. Oswald Chambers wrote, * "…faith brings us into right relationship with God and gives God his opportunity." God's opportunity comes many times in the midst of trouble and hard times when He appears to give us what seems to be a snake but actually He is preparing us to receive the gift of a fish. Then in the end, after faithfully enduring and willingness to give God his opportunity to grow us spiritually, our loving Heavenly Father opens His hand and shows us there really is a fish.

Many a battle-tested Christian will testify that when we do things God's way, even in the hard times, we will never be disappointed. The apostle Paul understood the point completely when he said, "Fight the good fight of faith". (1Timothy 6:12) I believe he must have swung a few spiritual diplors in his life as well!

*Oswald Chambers, "My Utmost for His Highest"
Copyright, 1935 by Dodd, Mead & Company, Inc. p. 305

DAY 7

PORK CHOP

Like most southern states, Georgia is made up of many small towns built around their life-sustaining rural highways or railroad tracks. Good Hope is just such a town, huddled close to Highway 83 in the beautiful farmlands of Georgia. Also, like many other small southern towns, it is made up of the infamous "good ole boys."

Why grown men are called "good ole boys" is strange because everything they do is not always 100-percent good. Like everyone else, they are occasionally guilty of wrongdoing ranging from kicking the dog to downright breaking the law. No doubt, every good ole boy that is a hunter or fisherman has been guilty of committing both of these crimes at least one time or another.

One pair of good ole boys, Siddard and Tiny, visited Good Hope often because Siddard's dad owned a farm there. The farm was a great place for hunting but it was particularly good during dove season.

The two men were typical of most dedicated hunters. They had a high standard of priorities and hunting was always at the top regardless of anything else going on in their lives. Tiny and Siddard wanted dove season this particular year to be a year remembered, so they talked Siddard's dad into letting them bait a field.

To the non-hunter who does not understand the term, "bait a field", it is really quite simple. The hunter throws a little grain on top of the soil in the field a few weeks before the dove season opens. The grain looks like hors d'oeuvres to the dove flying above and of course it attracts the dove and all their friends. But, because baiting a field is illegal, it may attract the game warden and all his friends as well. Siddard and Tiny rationalized the whole idea by reciting the universal naughty kid phrase, "Ah Pa, everybody does it."

Pa Siddard had a 50-acre cotton field and he reluctantly agreed to let the boys bait the middle of it. The cotton stalks were almost waist-high so it would be ideal for a baited field.

Opening day for dove season finally arrived and all three men were in the field for the shoot. It was great! It looked as if doves were flying in from three counties around. The hour finally arrived for the season to start and the shoot began with shotguns exploding around the perimeter of the field and doves falling in the middle. Their guns were smoking, the men were chewing, spitting and sweating and the dogs stayed busy retrieving the kill.

But wouldn't you know it? Just when these good ole boys were having a good ole time, suddenly speeding around the field comes not one---but two--green pick-up trucks filled with game wardens.

Pa Siddard saw them first and hollered, "Game warden! Run!" and everybody did. Siddard and Tiny ran together in one direction around the field to the back of the farm and Pa ran in another direction out toward the middle of the cotton field.

Pa knew he was not young enough or fast enough to outrun the game wardens so he ran until he was sucking air and felt his lungs would burst, so he just squatted down underneath the limbs of the cotton branches and fell over in a heap. He felt reasonably sure the game wardens could not see him as long as he stayed low and still, so he froze.

His plan might have worked except for Jake, his lifetime friend and pointer bird dog, who began to trail his scent. He worked a zigzag trail across the field with his tail flagging high above the cotton plants, following the familiar scent of his favorite companion. Pa looked up through the cotton stalks and saw what Jake was doing so he frantically grabbed dirt clods and began to throw them at the dog. He whispered in a raspy voice as loud as he dared, "Get out of here, Jake!" Nothing doing. A good dog stays with the trail and Jake soon zoned Pa in and ran right up to him and sat down. He looked lovingly at Pa with his long pink tongue hanging out the side of his mouth as he panted against the heat.

The game wardens saw Jake and knew what he was doing so with little effort they made their first arrest of the day.

Meanwhile, Siddard and Tiny circled the farm. They were frantically looking for a place to hide. As they came around the pigpen they knew they had to find cover fast because they could hear the game wardens closing in. The nearest cover was a pig shed, so they ran for it.

As they jumped over the fence into the pigpen, they slipped and slid awkwardly to sidestep pigs and mud holes and made their way to the shed. Tiny reached the pig shed first, dropped to his knees and crawled in with Siddard close behind him. A fat, young pig occupying the shed squealed in surprise as the two men squeezed into the small shelter and became temporary roommates.

The footsteps of running men outside could be heard nearing the pens so Siddard quickly grabbed the pig and thrust him into the door so the game wardens could not see inside the shed. Siddard held onto the squirming pig's hind legs to keep it from escaping.

The game wardens walked by searching the area, but only briefly glanced at the fat pig that stood squealing in the door of the shed.

Siddard and Tiny remained quietly in their hiding place for some time despite the pungent odor and their cramped positions. Finally, when all was quiet they decided to take a chance and come out of hiding. They painfully straightened their stiff bodies and attempted to brush off as much of the filth as they dared touch. They quietly walked around the back of the barn and cautiously moved to the corner to see if they could get a safe view of the dove field. They peered carefully around the corner of the barn just in time to see the game wardens cuff Pa, tuck him respectfully in the truck and take him off to jail.

After the last truck left and the dust settled, Siddard and Tiny walked out toward the deserted dove field. Siddard thrust his hands deep into his camouflaged pants and contemplated the day's events, part of that contemplation being a whole new appreciation for pork chops.

Slowly he glanced sideways at Tiny and said, "What do you think we ought to do, finish the dove shoot or go get Pa out of jail?" The vote was unanimous and they reluctantly unloaded their guns and headed for the house.

> ***"If you love me, you will keep my commandments."***
> ***John 14:15***

Many things motivate us to obey rules and laws in our society today...loss of driver's license if we speed in our cars, receiving an expensive fine if we cheat on our income-tax, or a jail sentence if we embezzle the company funds. In order to control lawlessness and dishonesty in our land, the law enforcement system takes away the things most important to us---money, freedom, rights and social acceptance.

However, this is not a perfect system because everyday lawbreakers still manage to escape being caught and convicted, despite the efforts of Sheriff Bubba and sharp-minded District Attorneys. So of course, it is the possibility of not being caught or convicted that continues to motivate lawlessness.

What will keep the dens of iniquity from developing and prospering among the people? Jesus had the answer in the Gospel of John when He said simply in less than ten words, "If you love me, you will keep my commandments."

Is this a joke? The walls of our judicial system are filled with hundreds of dusty volumes of commanding laws that are complicated enough to confuse a Philadelphia lawyer and yet criminals still get away with murder. So how can this simple commandment that Jesus gave us work to develop obedience in a person's life?

The answer is in the word "love". Humanly speaking it is difficult to understand how this kind of love relationship is possible. How is it possible to love in a degree that we would willingly obey laws without a police force patrolling our lives to keep us in check? The nearest human knowledge we have of this kind of love is love between parent and child. But as much as a child loves his parents, he has on many occasions broken the rules the parents set for him. So how can we love deeply enough to refrain from breaking laws?

The love that John is talking about is the agape love of which Jesus is the source. This is a love that is complete and everlasting and does not fall out of love as the human love can. Agape love is fully-committed, unconditional, not with-holding and is totally absorbed and focused on infusing the character of Jesus into an individual's life.

In order to have agape love we have to know the source and that requires spending time with the provider. It is impossible to love someone unless we spend time with them and learn who they are. We will find that as we spend time with God in His word and in prayer we will learn that our very purpose in life is to be in His presence, to be aware of Him constantly and to be in complete oneness with Him.

A thought worthy of expressing this says, "I yearn to feel God's presence...so real it takes my breath away, so divine it devastates me, and so gracious and loving it melts my defenses."* This is a love relationship with God that makes it possible in our flesh to obey Him completely. This is a love that is more passionate than law, obedient beyond commandment and is taught through the presence of the Holy Spirit who dwells in us as believers.

And how does the Scripture tell us that God returns His love to us in just one of many, many ways? "For the eyes of the Lord move to and fro throughout the earth that He may strongly support those whose heart is completely His. (2 Chronicles 16:9) Thank You, Father, for sending your Son, Jesus, so the agape love can be expressed through our lives by the power of the indwelling Holy Spirit.

*Constance Windhorst, PROGRESS September 91, pg. 16.

CALL OF THE WILD

It has always been interesting how little boys like to play grown up men and grown up men like to play little boys. No matter what the age they pull on the camouflage greens, grab their guns, (pretend or real) call up their dogs and head for the woods.

I have learned that after spending adequate time in the woods satisfying their yearnings for the wild and nurturing their male bonding---these little, big boys---come home smelling and sounding like what they are hunting as well.

Part of the thrill of the hunt is the skill to mimic the animals and birds they are hunting. There are a number of strange devices to select from to accomplish this art. One in particular that my Daniel Boone husband uses is a strange device that he places in his mouth and blows into and with practice he can sound like most anything that moves around in the woods. It takes hours to learn how to do this---just sitting around blowing into these strange things until he gets the hang of it.

One rainy winter day, after taking care of endless errands, car-pooling the children in five o'clock traffic and putting up with a lot of general aggravation, I finally arrived home. I had developed quite an attitude and was looking for any old dog to kick.

As I opened the front door and fell into our foyer with all my packages and three hungry, argumentative children behind me, I heard the most horrible noise I had ever heard. I did not have to be a rocket scientist to figure out that Mike was experimenting with a new wild game call. He was pushed back in his recliner with newspapers around him on the floor and an empty can of soda and a sack of chips scattered on a table beside him. He was the picture of a comfortable, contented man and in his camouflaged clothing he favored a happy green tree.

Pretending interested, I walked haughtily into the room where he was practicing. Angrily shaking the rain from my raincoat I snapped, "Well, what are you learning to be today?" My eyebrow over my right eye shot upward, almost parting my hair.

Talking around the device in his mouth he said, "I'm a turkey!" An innocent smile came and went quickly on the lips in training.

I was in a mood to do some target practice with my attitude so I replied sarcastically, "Well, you don't need much practice to accomplish that!"

Mike quickly spit the device into his hand and said defensively, "You don't understand, this is the hardest of all the fowl calls to mimic!"

I replied triumphantly over my shoulder on my way out of the room, "You must have accomplished it because it sure sounds foul to me." Bull's eye never felt so good.

But, woe is me; Mike was fast on the draw. He returned the volley quickly, "Well it sure attracted your foul mood." Then he broke into gales of laughter and raised his soda can in a mocking toast.

I left licking my wounds and looking for a limb to roost on. I knew I had fouled up.

He said to them, "But who do you say that I am?"
And Simon Peter answered and said, "Thou
art the Christ, the Son of the living God."
Matthew 16: 15, 16

Through the ages there have always been noises of counterfeit gods in the lives of mankind. It is quite common that these voices come from the things that are most important to man---career, success, material possessions, social life, hobbies and the list can go on and on.

But, of course, there is only one true God, Jehovah, and to know his voice we must first know Him.

According to any number of sources there are many ways to know God. The hunter and fisherman may say---to walk through the woods or sit by the water and see the wonder of His creation, is to know God. A mother would declare---to look into the face of a newborn baby and see the miracle of life, is to know God. To a frightened child--- God is the security he feels on a stormy night as he snuggles beneath his blankets. For the elderly---God is the relief from agony of pain caused by their aging bodies.

These are all examples of people who know about God, that He is creation, security and healer. But, who is God to each of us personally? Can we truly know His voice? Can we go beyond what He can do for us, deeper into what He can be to us personally?

In the scriptures in Matthew 16: 15, 16, Jesus spoke to a mighty fisherman, Simon Peter, and said, "But who do you say that I am?" Peter replied, "Thou art the Christ, the Son of the Living God."

Peter knew God. He knew Him through His Son, Jesus, and he also knew His voice through the sacred Word and the Holy Spirit he would receive later. Knowing all this enabled Peter to have a personal relationship with God, rather than just know about God.

Jesus asks each of us the same question He asked of Simon Peter, "But who do you say that I am?" Every man and woman will be accountable to answer that question one day. For those who reply "Thou art the Christ the Son of the living God," they have the privilege of entering into the most beautiful of all relationships possible...a personal relationship with Jesus Christ. Do you know His voice?

FUZZY WUZZY

Dove season was full-blown in Macon, Georgia and Durkee and Duke were in a hurry to get to the field. The field was 40 miles south of Macon by way of I-75 and from the interstate, they took to the rural roads.

Duke was driving the pick-up truck as they turned on a dusty road that led to the dove field. As they skirted the field, they were careful to stay off of the cultivated areas, so they bounced and rolled over some pretty rough terrain. At one point the trail narrowed and they had to pass under a pine tree with new, young growth hanging over the rough trail. They knew the truck could push through the tender young limbs without harm, so they continued down the narrow trail.

As they passed under the pine tree they suddenly realized the new growth had concealed large limbs that had been cut back to clear the trail. Too late to stop, the pick-up ran into one of the limbs and shattered the windshield.

The two men sat in the truck, stunned for a few seconds, staring at the shattered windshield and not believing the dumb thing they had done. The windshield was shattered so badly that visibility was impossible. How were they going to drive 40 miles home? And, of course, there was the dove field out there waiting for them.

The two discussed the situation briefly and came up with the most rational plan. They got out of the truck and Durkee looked around on the ground and found a four-foot limb with a gnarly knot near the end. He picked the limb up and took a big Hank Aaron swing into the windshield. Bang! He broke the windshield completely out of the truck. They raked the glass from the seat with bare hands, got back into the truck and drove on to the dove field to shoot. Typical of the attitude of most men in hunters camouflage, they come---they see---they conquer. Nothing keeps you from the hunt.

They had a pretty good shoot in the field. There were a fair number of doves flying. Even though they did not shoot their limit, they made some great shots. Eventually, they finished shooting and none too enthusiastically made their way back to the truck. They were dusty and hot but their newly ventilated truck could take care of both problems. There was no place in the immediate area to repair the truck windshield at the late hour so they decided to drive it back to Macon as it was.

Both men were still throwing glass out of the cab of the truck as they neared I-75. However, the drive had not been too bad on the backcountry roads, mostly because they could not go very fast. As they pulled on to I-75 and picked up speed it was a different story. When the speedometer hit the speed limit on the open road, they were holding onto their hats and squinting their eyes hard against the rush of wind.

Despite the uncomfortable circumstances, the two men tried to make the best of the situation as they recalled the details of the dove shoot that day. But the noise of the wind was so loud they were yelling their conversation back and forth between each other.

Durkee was particularly enjoying reliving a lucky shot he had made and turned his head toward Duke to enjoy a good laugh about it. About the time he threw his head back and opened his mouth to deep belly laugh, a fuzzy three-inch moth hit him dead center in the mouth.

Due to the speed of the truck, the moth hit his mouth with such velocity that it did not slow down until it hit his tonsils. Durkee had no choice in the matter---he had to swallow to keep from chocking and the frantic flapping of wings inside his mouth was more than he could stand.

From the driver's side of the truck, Duke saw his friend's body jerk, and suddenly go into a spasm. He was kicking the dash wildly, beating his chest and choking with saliva foaming up in his mouth as his body was drawn into a fetal position. Jerking the steering wheel and braking wildly Duke yelled in alarm, "Man, what's wrong?" Durkee, red-faced and gagging with tears running from his bulging eyes finally croaked out, "I swallowed a moth, I reckon."

Suddenly, Durkee thrust both feet onto the floor of the truck and he strained forward in his seat with his head between his knees. He kept trying to swallow because he was afraid he could not face what he might throw up. And if he did throw up it was going to plaster Duke and himself with slimy mucus because the wind was blowing so hard through the walloped windshield.

Involuntarily, he gagged again, swallowed hard and gasped, "For all I know it could have been a bat!" Eventually Durkee's body settled down and decided to digest the protein meal that had been thrust into it. This experience seemed to be just another life lesson on the consequences of trying to swallow more than you can chew.

"And the Lord appointed a great fish to swallow Jonah and Jonah was in the stomach of the fish three days and three nights.
Jonah 1:17 and Jonah 2: 1-10

God had a plan for Jonah to go to a city called Nineveh to become a part of greatly needed work there. The people of Nineveh were wicked and God wanted Jonah to go and tell them to repent or God would place His judgment on them. The scripture tells us that Jonah did not like the plan God had for him so Jonah came up with a plan of his own. But God *always* has the best plan for us so in order for God to get Jonah's attention He allowed Jonah to be swallowed by a fish during the pursuit of his own mindset and disobedience.

The scripture tells us that God appointed a great fish to swallow Jonah. Our comment to this story might be, "Well, if I were in Jonah's shoes I would be too smart to be swallowed by a fish." Maybe so, but at one time or another because of rebellion or disobedience, most of us have ended up as someone else's lunch. We deliberately turn away from the plan God has for us, devise our own plan and later find ourselves swallowed by the consequences of disobedience. The wrong plan or the right plan at the wrong time has a way of eating away our best opportunities.

You will also notice that not only was Jonah in the belly of the great fish, but the seaweed was literally wrapping around him. (Jonah 2:5) This is a plan really gone bad!

But notice in chapter two how Jonah found the exit sign to escape from the fish's stomach:

(1) Jonah realized he must repent for disobedience, "Then Jonah prayed to the Lord his God from the stomach of the fish, and he said, "I called out of distress to the Lord, and He answered me."(Jonah 2: 1, 2)

(2) Jonah realizes his sin, sees his helplessness and accepts the fact that God has something better for him. From Jonah's perspective things could not have been worse as we see in verse 4, "So I have been expelled from Thy sight..." and verse 5, "Water encompassed me to the point of death." Jonah's life looked like a disaster. But because of repentance, everything in the heavenly realm changed.

From God's perspective, repentance from Jonah became an opportunity for Jonah to grow spiritually and serve again. God says in Ezekiel 18:32, "For I have no pleasure in the death of anyone who dies," declares the Lord God. "Therefore, repent and live." What a loving God we have who is so willing to forgive, restore and grant us another chance.

Is your life beginning to smell a little fishy and the "whale of a time" isn't such a big time after all? Try chapter two of Jonah.

DAY 10

A WEAPON IS
A WEAPON

A pioneer woman was expected to stand on the line and protect her children, home and property while her husband was away looking for provision for his family. Out of her own resourcefulness she had to fight off Indian attacks and creatures from the wild and deal with natural disasters until he returned.

The same situation is pretty much true today in our modern society. Many husbands are still traveling to provide for their families, leaving their wives to protect the home front.

Fortunately, 911 has taken care of attacking intruders and Red Cross handles the natural disasters; but at our house, the wife still has to deal with the creatures from the wild.

Mike was out of town and the creature from the wild came in the form of a slithering, hissing cottonmouth snake. Our house, near a lake, attracted a lot of snakes but Mike had taught me to recognize the "good" snakes, or non-poisonous, and I left them alone to do their work. He also taught me to recognize the poisonous snakes and those I ran from screaming into the house.

This rule of respect held fine until the day one of the children left the basement door open and our yelping fox terrier warned me that a cottonmouth was about to crawl inside our house.

Terrified, I grabbed a hoe standing nearby and held the snake at bay. I thought I could handle him with this weapon until he opened his mouth and showed me his fangs and I saw the infamous cotton-white mouth all the way down to his toenails. The hoe then seemed more like a toothpick and this snake was in no mood for preventative dentistry.

My college-age daughter, Paige, and my visiting seventy-two year old mother came running across the deck above me and down the stairs when they heard me yelling for help.

"Run, get me a gun, quick," I told Paige and I kept staring at the two fangs and the white cotton lining of the snake's mouth. I knew he was maxed out on the irritation scale, so I did not dare move because I also knew this snake could become aggressive.

Mike had taught Paige and me how to handle and shoot his guns. I had fired his .22 rifle and the .410 shotgun on a number of occasions just in case this type of emergency arose. Paige enjoyed shooting with her dad, but after I hit a target a couple of times I felt there were quieter ways to entertain myself.

When Paige came running back across the deck above me and down the stairs, she handed me a pistol unlike the other guns I had practiced shooting. However, at the moment I was not shopping. I was too busy watching the snake. As far as I was concerned a gun is a gun, some are just longer than others. I learned later that a .357 Magnum is really a gun.

The thought crossed my mind that perhaps I should try this gun out by shooting into the lake. I remembered the stance that policewomen take on television, so I got myself into position, aimed at the five- acre lake and fired. The gun sounded like a cannon and the noise was deafening, but I hit the lake.

When Paige and Mom heard the noise they threw their arms into the air, screamed and did a jig like Laurel and Hardy on the silent movies and retreated halfway up the deck stairs.

With my ears still ringing, I decided to take care of the snake. I stood with my shoulder against the basement wall so I would not shoot the foundation out from under the house. I told Paige and Mom to go back up on the deck in case there was a ricochet. They turned and ran back up the stairs and stomped across the deck above me. My mother, who stood all of four feet and ten inches, was having no problem maneuvering, considering the motivation. She moved like a track star.

I aimed at the open mouth of the enemy and fired. The explosion of the gun was trapped beneath the deck and all I could hear was a massive roar.

Paige and Mom were still standing above me and after I fired, I heard them scream and do the Laurel and Hardy shuffle again. Then they stomped back across the deck and down the stairs. Their steps sounded strange though, kind of like I was hearing them under water.

The snake was wounded and charging. "Go back upstairs," I yelled at them, "I'm going to shoot again."

Back up the 15 stairs the granddaughter and grandmother ran and I heard them again stomp across the deck above me. Their steps still sounded as if I was underwater, but I did not have time to think about that.

I aimed again and fired. The noise of the gun exploded for a third time under the deck and roared in my ears, but this time I conquered my prey. Above me I could barely hear the muffled screams and shuffles of Mom and Paige doing their matinee performance. Their running footsteps back across the deck and down the stairs were scarcely audible and I was not aware of their presence until I looked around and saw them standing behind me.

The three of us stood around the twisting body of the dying snake. Mom and Paige were pointing to the snake and making facial expressions and I thought they were doing more of their silent movie antics because their lips were moving but no sound was coming out of their mouths, or none that I could hear.

Three days later I was finally able to hear a telephone ring, hear someone call me from another room and hear Mike explain to me why you don't use a .357 Magnum to protect yourself from a snake.

Then David said to the Philistine, "You come to
me with a sword, a spear and a javelin, but I come
to you in the name of the Lord of hosts, the God of
the armies of Israel, whom you have taunted."
I Samuel 17:45

Don McIntyre's visit in Europe was not exactly one described in trendy travel brochures. He landed on the coast of France on D-Day during World War II and walked all the way to Germany. The M-1 rifle he carried was almost as big as he was since he did not weigh but 145 pounds soaking wet, which was most of the time.

He saw a lot of young boys and men wounded and killed during this terrible time, but he escaped injury and used his round trip ticket home.

After the war, Don and his young family settled in a small community west of Rome, Georgia called Coosa. This is where Mike and his parents became friends with the McIntyre family. Don and his wife, Pauline, owned and operated a small convenience store near Coosa High School where Mike went to school and played football for the Coosa Eagles. Both families were very involved in the community church that was rich in God's love.

Don volunteered to teach the boys' high school Sunday school class which was the class Mike attended. No one else wanted this class because high school boys can be rudely uninterested when it comes to teaching them the truths from the Bible. At this age, they sometimes think they are tougher and smarter than anybody and completely invincible. Just one innocent mistake from the teacher and control can be lost to catcalls, cocky strutting and general disrespect. The possibility that this could happen never seemed to bother Don, and Pauline was always by his side to encourage and assist if she was needed.

Don was a good teacher in a simple kind of way. He had a knack for sharing the scripture through his life personally so that it grabbed the boys' attention and held it. The way he told the Bible stories made the boys feel as if they were a part of the story.

It was a lot like Don's tales of the war. He was in the battle so he knew from experience how the battle went and could convey that excitement and experience to them.

And there was always Pauline with him in the room, eager to look up a scripture and read it for Don when he needed it.

There was never any disrespect from these boys, even though they laughed a lot at Don's poking fun at them and his lighthearted humor. But as spirited as they were they always gave their full attention to Don when he got into the scriptures. You could hear a pin drop as he shared God in his life and he allowed the boys to see his heart.

After Mike left Coosa and was out of college and working, he was visiting his parents while on a business trip. He and his mom were enjoying catching up on local news and news from the church. Of course, Mike finally got around to asking about Don and how his old Sunday school class was doing. Mike shared with his mom how much he missed Don and felt sure Don was the best Sunday school teacher he ever had.

He glanced at his mother as he finished the comment and saw a slight smile on her lips. Curious, Mike asked her what she was smiling about. His mother looked at him, smiled again and said, "Well I suppose its okay for you to know now. Do you know that Don McEntire cannot read?"

Startled Mike could not imagine that this could be true. Then instantly flooding back across Mike's mind came the picture of Pauline always in the class at Don's side, looking up verses in the Bible and reading the scripture. How much more precious Don's teaching was to Mike in that moment knowing that he had allowed himself to become completely vulnerable before teenage boys, so that he could teach God's Word.

Looking back on this situation Mike knew that God could have called in heavy weaponry to teach that class, and from man's perspective, the class would need it. God could have nudged a professional teacher with a degree or even a deputy sheriff to teach the class, both were in the church and their presence in the room would have brought the boys into submission.

But no, God needed a David with his slingshot and Don was there. Don's slingshot was loaded with the same awesome ammunition David's was loaded with…a love for the Lord and a desire to serve Him.

This was an important lesson to Mike…to take every opportunity to thank the Don McIntyre's who fight for the homeland and the "heart land" and the spouses who stand beside them.

Thank you Don and Pauline.

DOGS, CARS AND OTHER STUFF

Life is filled with a great deal of collection,
Day after day a very steady selection.
Fishing poles, guns and a dog for my spouse;
Antiques, new china and a rug for the house.

There's skill in shopping, knowing just where to
buy,
A polite turn on the heel if the price is too high.
Some items are valuable, the other just stuff;
Heavens, stop us, when enough is enough!

DAY 11

WHAT'S SO FUNNY?

Residents of the northern part of our country use the words, "Down South" as if the south was another country or continent, and to some perhaps it is. But to others the words have a charm that instantly bring to mind the smell of magnolias, lazy summer afternoons and a style of living that people do not understand unless they have lived it. Perhaps this is what lures the northern population down for frequent visits leaving their foul weather and fast-paced living. But along with the great climate and delightful slow drawls---the anticipation of southern cooking has long been the lure of the south.

Growing up in the south I had ample opportunity to gain first-hand experience with our great southern cooking. My parents owned a small diner off of Highway 82 in a little town called Gordo about 25 miles west of Tuscaloosa, Alabama. This was a great location because this was the route many northerners traveled on their journey south.

As a teenager I worked in the diner as a waitress during the summers. My work could have been extremely boring except for the snow birds that stopped by for a hot meal on their way to more exciting places. They came in hungry and ready to excite their taste buds with our down-home cooking.

Make no mistake; I was a country girl who had never traveled more than a hundred miles in any direction. To hear those Yankees' conversations in their crisp brogues talk about their travels was more excitement than I saw in a year of Sundays.

However, as country as I was, I had my pride. I loved to take advantage of any opportunity to show those yanks how couth and refined this southern belle was. I tried hard to impress them with my knowledge of southern cuisine and my sophisticated demeanor nurtured during all fifteen years of my very experienced life.

A favorite dish on the menu was my mother's Brunswick stew. Not a breathing soul in Pickens County could hold a candle to her succulent mixture and she would not dare tell the recipe because, "I'll have to shoot 'em," she would chuckle and say. She would work for days cooking up a new pot of this savory mixture of chicken, pork, vegetables and spices. My dad always said it was a three hummer, "um, um, umuh!"

I remember one day in particular I had served orders of the stew to a table of tourists from Michigan. I was a bit pompous and proud as I sat the bowls of steaming stew in front of each guest; I was sure they had never tasted anything so wonderful. They immediately began to spoon in mouthfuls of the tasty delight and I watched as their palates approved and they hunkered down to get serious with the meal.

One of the tourists with his mouth full asked me crisply, "May I have some saltines, Sugar?" I stared down my nose at him a full five seconds, then I replied in a syrupy drawl, "Sur, we don't have any saltines." The tourist's spoon was on its way to his mouth when his hand stopped and he asked, "What do you usually eat with your stew?" I lifted my chin high enough to get frostbite and answered, "We eat crackers."

Twenty five miles west of Tuscaloosa on Highway 82, I'd never heard a cracker called a saltine.

As I turned and left the table, the man's spoon was frozen in mid air and his mouth was still open.

Back in the kitchen, I heard an explosion of laughter coming from the dining area and I wondered what those hungry tourists from Detroit could have experienced in their travel's that was so funny. I thought to myself, "They probably would not know a real knee-slapper if it was right in front of their noses."

> *"Why do you spend money for what is not bread and your wages for what does not satisfy? Listen carefully to me and eat what is good and delight yourself in abundance. Isaiah 55:2*

Food has always been important to mankind, obviously, for survival and enjoyment. In fact, food and man's need for it is so important that references are made numerous times in the scriptures, particularly in the New Testament. The gospel writers make notice of the many opportunities Jesus had to feed those around Him.

However, God knew man would not always be content with satisfying his basic need for food. The desires of the flesh are many and man's appetite runs rampant and many times out of control with desires for more and more satisfying stuff.

Eventually, after accumulating more stuff and having one more new experience, man begins to realize that none of this satisfies for any length of time, but he is caught in a vicious cycle... trying one new thing after another.

God in His infinite wisdom knew this would happen so he used Isaiah as his mouthpiece to say, "Why do you spend money for what is not bread, and your wages for what does not satisfy?" Mankind spends much of his time and money seeking things to feed and satisfy the flesh when actually it is the spirit that is starving to death.

God has an abundant table for man to feast upon so that the whole man can be fed. The table offers a personal relationship with His Son, Jesus Christ, intimacy with the Holy Spirit and a well of wisdom from His Word. In comparison to what the world has to offer as food, this table is the crème de la crème and much, much more.

And let it not go unnoticed that for all who are concerned with healthy eating, God's food is not high in cholesterol so there is no danger of heart attack. In fact, this food has been known to heal man's heart and make it pure and good (see Proverbs 17:22). His food is not full of sugar, so there is no danger of gaining weight. But this food from God's table has a taste so sweet that it takes away the bitterness of life because it is sweeter than honey and the honeycomb (see Psalms 19:10). Although it is full of salt it will not affect the blood pressure (see Colossians 4:6) but will season our walk so others notice as we go about our lives. And the content of vitamins and iron are so high that it gives strength to meet our daily tasks (see 1 Corinthians 4:10).

God is in the feeding and providing business and He desires to feed the whole man completely. But we should be willing to eat what God provides and follow His complete menu. As Isaiah said, "Listen carefully to me and eat what is good and delight yourself in abundance."

DAY 12

THE CAR

It is interesting how many Americans' first expression of successful living is made by the purchase of the car. *The car* says, I have made the promotion, have been given the raise and I am on my way to the top of the corporate ladder.

I remember very clearly our big statement purchase was a 1957 Cadillac. To a lot of people that sounds impressive but the calendar on our wall at the time read 1965 and... the Cadillac was pink.

The purchase was an even greater problem because *the car* was a dream of Mike's and a nightmare of mine. I wanted a new yellow Volkswagen like many of our friends were zipping around in. And actually, that was about all we could handle financially on our particular rung of the corporate ladder.

We were visiting Mike's parents in Centre, Alabama when the controversial purchase was made. The owner convinced Mike that this was a deal he could not afford to pass up and that I would be tickled the same color as the Cadillac about the whole thing. My first knowledge of the purchase came at Mike's parents' front door when he pulled into their driveway. When I realized we were the proud owners of the pink monstrosity, a two-humped camel would have been more inviting transportation.

To say I was not pleased with the purchase of *the car* was an understatement. And, of course, being in his parent's home for the weekend did not give me an opportunity to really let him know how I felt, because how I felt was going to get loud. Mike was walking a wide path around me and I was trying to be polite to his parents but inside I was a volcano ready to blow.

The strained weekend eventually came to an end and Mike, excited about driving the giant bottle of Pepto Bismol disguised as a car back to Athens, began to get our bags ready and was loading them in *the car*. I balked, threw myself into a chair, crossed my arms and insisted that I would not be caught in his pink pretense of prosperity.

Little beads of sweat began to roll down the sides of Mike's face as he kissed his mom goodbye and shook hands with his dad. He then walked over to my chair, picked me up, gently tossed me over his shoulder, walked outside to *the car* and placed me in the passenger side of his dream buggy and closed the door. Before he could walk around to his side of *the car*, I opened my door, got out and slammed it shut then stomped back into the house to my chair. He followed me and repeated the ritual again and this time when he placed me in *the car*, he held me down and climbed over me into the driver's side of *the car* in case I made a break back into the house again. He started the engine and we pulled out of the drive.

Mike's parents tried to be tactful and control their facial expressions, but as we pulled out of the driveway, gales of laughter could be heard coming from the porch.

Back in Athens, according to Martha, *the car* did not fit into our household any better than it had in Alabama. I refused to allow Mike to drop me off in front of the bank where I worked. Nobody at the bank drove a Cadillac but the president and his was black. I insisted on being dropped off two blocks away and I walked to the bank, rain or shine.

I was almost at my wit's end when finally the victory blow came. Mike had three magnificent obsessions. His first was hunting and fishing the second was owning fancy cars and the third… he loved to eat.

On my very first trip to the grocery store, the bag boy carrying my groceries to *the car*, took one look at it and said, "Your great aunt died and left it to you… right?" I refused to go grocery shopping in *the car* again. After a week of eating nothing but Rice Krispies and peanut butter and jelly sandwiches, *the car* was returned. This again proves the brilliant military strategy that man travels on his stomach and not in *the car*.

> **"Search me, oh God, and know my heart; Try me and know my anxious thoughts; and see if there be any hurtful way in me, and lead me in the everlasting way." Psalm 139: 23, 24**

A classic, "What is the difference between" joke begins, "What is the difference between an angry woman and a pit bulldog?" The answer… "lipstick."

Very funny, and if someone examined the joke book hall of fame, they would certainly find one just as funny for men.

Every man and woman on numerous occasions has indulged themselves with a hateful attitude, a difference of opinion and certainly with the loss of temper. In order to avoid an ulcer or strained relationship as a result of these indulgences, we should go to God's Word and get an attitude adjustment.

The Bible has many examples of people who had attitude adjustments. No one is exempt from relationship problems and differing opinions and the enemy will certainly make sure that we get more than our fair share of them. And so as not to give the devil more credit than he is worth (because he is a defeated foe) often we simply indulge in these attitudes because we choose to be controlled by undisciplined decisions to satisfy the flesh. Take a look at the great apostle Paul for example. There are several examples of relationship clashes in his life, even with his close friends and work companions. Had he not resolved them, they would have stunted his effectiveness for God's service.

David, the author of Psalm 139, is another example of one who allowed a "hurtful way" to manifest itself in his heart and it led to tragedy. But fortunately his spirit was grieved of his wrongdoing and David's heart was broken with remorse and he allows us to see that brokenness in the scripture. Through David's example, God shows us how we are to respond to anger, anxiety and hurtful ways; "Point out anything in me that offends you, and lead me along the path of everlasting life." (Psalm 139:24 New Living Bible)

David says, "Search my heart, Lord." How many times have we put on a sweet face for someone yet in our hearts we would like to punch their lights out? God knows when our heart is filled with anger and anxious thoughts, so we should allow

God through the convicting of the Holy Spirit dwelling in us to search out those hidden places that are fuming behind the seemingly pleasant face.

An offended attitude (which is Satan's finest weapon) can lead to irrational action and if not checked can make life pretty miserable. A wise, unknown author once said, "There is no such thing as a happy, disobedient Christian. There is also no such thing as an unhappy, obedient Christian."

When we allow God to search our hearts and help us change the hurtful ways, He can point us toward the everlasting way. The everlasting way can begin today if we have the heart for it.

DAY 13

SAY WHAT?

After hearing the explosion of too many guns fired and passing the big 40, Mike realized he definitely had a hearing problem and needed to look into the possibility of a hearing aid.

During this period of his life when "huh" was the most frequently used word in his vocabulary, there were many warning signs that strongly suggested his hearing capacity was in trouble. One of the warning signs was obvious when we visited places with a great deal of noise such as a noisy restaurant; this was torment of the worst kind. In this kind of atmosphere, in order to hear a conversation he would have to sit forward in his chair, lean across the table, cup his ear in his hand and strain to hear each word.

One particular occasion Mike and I were dining in a restaurant with our good friends, Jerry and his wife, Lou. Unfortunately, Jerry had a similar hearing problem for the same reason Mike did. The only difference was that Jerry was older than Mike by twelve years so he had heard a decade more shells shot than Mike.

The two men sat across the table from each other, excitedly carrying on a conversation. They appreciated the same things in life and enjoyed each other's company enormously so exchanging hunting and fishing stories was a delicacy to be savored. Both were sitting forward in their offensive hearing positions, hands cupped behind the ear and habitually grunting, "Huh? Huh?" as they grinned and nodded in agreement with each other. They strained hard to hear and be heard above the restaurant noise.

Lou and I, also sitting across the table from each other, strained our ears to hear the direction of the men's conversation. Between their "huh's?" and repeated sentences two or three times, it took serious concentration. We turned our heads from one man to the other as if watching a tennis match, listening intently, puzzled by changes of direction in their conversation subject as they conversed back and forth. Suddenly, we realized that in the noisy room the two men, unable to hear each other clearly, were talking about two completely different subjects. Lou and I made a quick exit to the ladies room and came unglued with laughter. It was an experience we have long remembered.

Fortunately, Mike and I had an acquaintance in the hearing aid business so we called and asked if he could come by our home to discuss the matter of Mike's hearing loss. He explained that he could do some preliminary tests to see if Mike was a candidate for a hearing aid. On the evening that he came he worked quite a while testing Mike to determine his hearing level.

Eventually he was ready for Mike to try a test with a sample hearing aid. Mike attached the aid and was immediately overwhelmed by the onslaught of sounds that he could hear. He could hear sounds he had not heard for years---frogs croaking, crickets chirping, and the TV at a normal volume level. He was so excited that large beads of sweat began forming on his forehead and temples and began sliding down each side of his face.

To further test the distance capacity of the aid, I was instructed to stand with my back to Mike and begin walking into the other room talking in a normal voice as I walked away from him. As I walked I began asking him questions. "Mike, do you want to go fishing?" "Yeah, yeah," he replied and followed with an excited, "Hey, I can hear you!" I continued to walk away from him talking. "Do you want to go quail hunting?" I asked. "I sure do, he grinned. Man, this is great. I hear you, keep walking," he said. He was grinning from ear to ear and the sweat continued to pour.

A theory I had wanted to test for years came to mind. Rather than walking farther away, I stopped in the place he last heard me and asked, "Mike, do you want to clean up the dinner dishes for me?" Mike suddenly began to slap at the hearing aid and a scowl came over his face as he pulled out a handkerchief and wiped the sweat from his face. "Something must be wrong with this thang...suddenly I can't hear nothin'!"

This was confirmation to me that fifty percent of Mike's hearing problem was hearing loss and fifty percent was hearing only what he wanted to hear.

"Now when they heard this, they were pierced to the hearts and said to Peter and the rest of the Apostles, "Brethren, what shall we do?" Acts 2:37

What we hear and how we react to what we hear can determine important directions in our lives and the lives of our families and loved ones as well. This was the case with this huge crowd of men in Jerusalem who gathered to hear Peter's sermon on the day of the Pentecost feast. Not one among them realized that this was the day the church was being birthed and the powerful arrival of the Holy Spirit into the life of the believer.

It began with Peter's first sermon after the baptism of the Holy Spirit in the upper room. One hundred and twenty believers also waited in that room with Peter for the Holy Spirit to come upon them with the baptism of power as Jesus had instructed earlier before He ascended into heaven.

Peter's sermon was so powerful that hundreds of men and women listening could not walk away; they were mesmerized in awe of the words they heard. The scripture says, "they were pierced to the hearts" and the piercing convicted them to ask, "Brethren, what shall we do?" The question directed them to make the most important decision of their lives. That decision was to understand their need to receive Jesus Christ as their Savior and to receive the gift of the Holy Spirit.

The next scripture in verse 39 tells us that a precious promise was given to the men as a result of hearing and acting upon what they heard. It says, "For the promise is for you and your children and for all who are far off, as many as the Lord our God shall call to Himself." So we see that as a result of parents' decisions to receive Jesus as Savior, our children, grandchildren, great grandchildren (and generations afterwards) will also have the opportunity to know Jesus Christ as well.

Is there any promise more important to any man or woman? The promise of seeing our off- spring receive Jesus Christ as Savior because they hear parents declare a testimony of who

He is in their lives. There is no greater heritage that we parents can give our children. And not only for our children but friends and acquaintances outside our family "all who are far off," the scripture tells us as well.

A beautiful gift God has given man is the ability to hear, but hearing His voice through the "piercing of the heart" that can result in godly *action* and *reaction* is the most beautiful gift of all.

BETTER WATCH OUT, BETTER NOT POUT

Someone once said, "It's not who you are, it's who you know" and Mike has certainly lived this out in his life. His sanguine personality is always on the alert to others around him and he is never in company with anyone very long before he becomes well-acquainted with them. Consequently, the number of people he knows is quite large in comparison to an average person's list of friends and acquaintances. So naturally it never fails, if we are across town having dinner in a restaurant or at Disney World in Florida on vacation, Mike always runs into someone he knows.

One year during the Christmas season, Mike was in the local mall doing his Christmas shopping. As he left a department store he was pleasantly surprised by a beautiful life-size Christmas wonderland in the promenade. The setting was complete with Santa's helpers and Santa sitting in his chair, ready to receive starry-eyed children with their Christmas lists. Apparently there was a lull in business because Santa was all alone, not a child in sight.

As Mike skirted the holiday setting and continued to window shop, he heard someone yelling, "Hey Mike, how are you doing?" Mike stopped and looked around slowly at the busy shoppers. He saw no one he knew, so he continued walking.

Again he heard a voice, "Hey Mike!" He stopped a second time, looked around for a familiar face, and then realized to his surprise that it was Santa Claus yelling to him.

Mike was embarrassed that Santa knew his name so he looked around at the shoppers one more time to make sure no one was watching.

Reluctantly he looked at Santa and asked the most embarrassing question of his life, "Are you talking to me?" and he thumped himself in the chest with his pointer finger.

Santa said, "You're Mike aren't you? Mike answered timidly, "Yes, but I don't know you."

"Sure you do, everybody knows Santa," replied the jolly fat man with a belly-jiggling chuckle.

Mike was now feeling even more ridiculous. "How do you know me?" he asked and like a child, rolled and unrolled the top of a shopping bag he was clutching in his hands.

"Santa knows everybody," was Santa's reply and sure enough, there was a twinkle in his eyes.

Then Mike detected a slight sound of familiarity in the slow drawl that came from the southern Santa, so he moved closer to get a better look. Seconds later he recognized the twinkle in the eyes was not from a mischievous jolly fat man from the North Pole, but from a colleague he had worked with several years earlier. The last time Mike had seen him he had a flat top and was clean-shaven. Now he had a naturally gray beard and long gray hair. He looked the perfect Santa Claus.

Mike and Santa stood in the winter wonderland and renewed their old friendship and they both laughed when Mike told Santa about the new shotgun he wanted Santa to bring him for Christmas. But as pleasant as this encounter had been, even Mike was a little taken a back that he had run into someone he knew from the North Pole.

> *But He answered and said, "Truly I say to you. I*
> *do not know you" Matthew 25:12 Living Bible*

Just as the statement "It's not who you are, it's who you know" is applicable in society today, it is most definitely true for eternity. Many people in our society spend today dreaming and working toward what will make them happy tomorrow and impress others around them. We think that if we know enough, earn enough, buy and collect enough it will open the door to everything we ever wanted. Not only will it give us physical and emotional happiness, we think, but also, it will hopefully impress the Joneses and make us "somebody." After all, everybody wants to be somebody and nobody wants to be just anybody.

Actually, there is nothing wrong with planning and setting goals for tomorrow as long as we take care of the things that are important today. The virgins in the scripture in Matthew 25:12 did neither and they found themselves left out in the darkness. We can find ourselves like the virgins if we keep putting off our salvation. This is a matter we must deal with today because Jesus said that He would return when we least expect it.

The Good News is we have nothing to fear for the present or future if we acknowledge in our head and our heart that God loved us so much that He sent His Son, Jesus, to die for our sins and made it possible for us to have eternal life (see John 3:16).

Also, we need to understand that every individual on earth has sinned and sin separates us from God (see Romans 3:23). In order for our relationship to be restored with God we must ask Him to forgive us for the sins in our lives.

Understanding these truths brings us to a most important decision---the decision to accept or reject Jesus Christ as Savior. We need to be mindful that putting off or making no decision at all is a decision of rejection. (John 12:48) Remaining neutral on this matter does not protect us in light of eternity. Perhaps now at this moment, you want to settle this matter if you are not sure where you will spend eternity. If that is the case, in the quietness of your heart simply pray, "Jesus, I believe you are the Son of God who died for my sins and made it possible for me to have eternal life. I also believe that according to the scriptures that on the third day after your death you arose from the grave and you are a living God. Jesus, I ask you to forgive me of my sins; I recognized that I have sinned but I desire to turn from that life. And now, I invite you into my life and I accept you as the Savior of my life. In Jesus' name, Amen."

Praying this prayer in faith makes it possible to know the King of kings and to become His child. So now, it is not only who you are, but whose you are.

DAY 15

WALKING THE DOG

The small print in my marriage license I did not read because I was too busy saying, "I do" and "I will" and generally the affirmative to everything. Had I read the small print I am sure it would have stated that I must have a chauffeur's license and be prepared to move out in a minivan at any moment in any direction to take care of household affairs. Even though I did not read the small print, I did gladly accept the responsibilities that are involved in transporting children to dentist, dance lessons, little league, birthday parties and all the numerous trips required in managing a family and running the household. However, there was one transporting responsibility I was not aware of and I was completely unprepared to handle.

"Take the dog to the vet." That is what Mike told me on the telephone…long distance. He was out of town and in his rush to leave early that morning he forgot to tell me one of his many dogs was sick and had to see the vet.

From my perspective Mike's occupation as a sales rep for the state of Georgia made it possible for him to have a dog in every town in Georgia. Having all these dogs strategically located in north, middle and south Georgia made it convenient for him to go hunting with a client when he was in that area. With so many dogs to care for I was not very sympathetic when one became ill.

"You can use my truck," as if that was on the top of my list of things that I always wanted to do and a trip to the Bahamas came next. "Simply put a rope through the collar, take her out of the pen and tie her in the bed of the truck," he said.

Much to my aggravation, I knew I had to take care of the matter, so I found the rope and went to the dog pens. It was then that I realized that with so many dogs in the pens I had no idea which of the six pointer bird dogs was Nell, the sick dog.

The dogs were all excited, of course, so I finally decided the dog that barked the weakest, jumped the lowest and ran the slowest had to be sick…so I took her.

I attached the rope to her collar and the moment I stepped outside the pen I knew I was wrong in my diagnostic stragedy of the animal. Nell bolted off so fast she jerked me out of my shoes and had me gasping for air when we reached the truck. Then I was mortified when I reached down to pick her up and put her in the truck. She bolted off again, jerking my arm out of the socket, forcing me to hurdle shrubs, lawn chairs, barbecue grills and split rail fences as I held onto her rope. After the sixth unsuccessful attempt to load her into the truck, I was exhausted and she was just getting revved up. My shins were bleeding and our yard looked as if a tornado had passed through it. I did not know what sickness this dog had, but at this point I was hoping she would drop dead from it.

I finally managed to get Nell into the truck bed and tied her behind the cab. I started the truck and drove toward the vet's office smelling of dog odor and spitting fur balls. I had driven only a short distance from our house when I glanced out the back window to check on her. All I could see was an empty truck bed and I knew instantly Nell had vacated the truck. I jerked my head around frantically trying to locate her when I noticed her rope was over the driver's side of the truck bed. I quickly slowed the truck and looked out my window. There was Nell, running along side the truck, her rope still holding her secure. Her tongue was hanging out of her mouth and she had a puzzled look on her face. She was accustomed to running all day on acres of grassy fields; but on hot asphalt...not so much fun.

I quickly stopped the truck and jumped out and untied the limp dog. I picked her up and put her in the cab with me. She was so exhausted she fell into a heap on the seat and never moved for the remainder of the trip.

After seeing the vet, Nell recovered from her illness and eventually recovered from her cross-country run. But after this adventure, Mike could never understand why one of his best dogs whined, balked and became wild every time he tried to load her into the truck.

> *"But a certain Samaritan who was on a journey came upon him, and when he saw him, he felt compassion." Luke 10:30-37*

Is it always convenient to minister to the unexpected, unplanned needs of others? In our busy society it seems everything must be on a calendar in advance in order to obtain attention from anyone. But nonetheless, usually when we are in our greatest hurry and in our most impatient attitude, the most unexpected opportunities to help others will arise.

This was the case with the Good Samaritan. He was likely on a business trip with his head filled with work-related problems and suddenly there was a man in need on the side of the road. We read where he *felt compassion* and he reacted with a mind-set ready to do the will of God. It appears the Samaritan man did not have to think about if he should help the fallen man or not…his reaction was to help him. The scripture following the Good Samaritan's initial discovery of the man in need gives a step-by-step account of his actions. It can easily be related to modern-day terminology.

First, he bandaged the man's wounds (attended the man until someone responded to 911). Second, he put him on his own beast (put the injured man in his own car or pick-up truck). Third, he brought him to an inn (motel) and fourth, took care of him (called the man's family, found him clean clothing and food). Last, the Samaritan told the innkeeper he would pay for any further cost (cash on the spot).

In our present day society, we are afraid to risk helping a stranger and with good reason because our days are indeed very wicked. But what about the people who live on our street, in our neighborhood, in our apartment complex and office building that we see everyday? We rush out our doors each morning and there are those within a stone's throw who are crying for help because of problems and pain in their lives. Like the man on the side of the road, they may be taking a beating from life either mentally, emotionally or physically and we are too busy to notice or help.

Perhaps we need to take the example of the Samaritan and allow our hearts to feel compassion and then act upon that compassionate feeling as it moves us to obedience. As Jesus said, "Truly I say to you, to the extent that you did it to one of these brothers of Mine; even the least of them, you did it to me." (Matthew 25:40) Allow the Holy Spirit to demonstrate the presence of Jesus in us as we move about on our journey each day and allow the prayer to be on our lips, "Lord, send me to someone who needs you.

WARRIOR ON I-85

Driving east on I-85 from Atlanta to Athens during rush-hour traffic with a fidgety three-year-old was reason enough to be nervous. To add to the pre-heart attack situation, I also had a brand new breakfast table and six chairs I had just purchased wedged into the bed of the small truck I was driving. The pieces that did not wedge into the bed were piled on top of the other furniture and tied. To test my mounting nervous tension the weather was threatening rain so the sales clerk at the furniture store tied a large tarpaulin over the furniture to keep it dry.

It was one of those cold, blustery February days and the blast from the wind and the 18-wheeler trucks on the interstate took turns blowing my small truck from one side of the road to the other. I felt as if we were in a cardboard box in the middle of an elephant stampede.

I had plenty to be anxious about as I drove home. The speeding, noisy traffic, the threatening weather, the furniture, and restless Angie in the seat next to me, all had me jumpy and nervous. But the tarpaulin tied around the furniture was the most nerve-wracking problem because the ropes kept jerking loose in the driving wind. And just as I feared, a few miles before my exit to Athens, I realized I would have to pull over on the busy expressway and secure the ropes or the flapping tarpaulin would become a driving hazard for other motorist.

Not accustomed to driving on a busy expressway, the thought of stopping beside the road and possibly inviting unwanted help had me hyperventilating. I had read many stories of unsolved mysteries about women who had disappeared on these busy expressways. But having no choice, I pulled over carefully and jumped out of the truck.

I was completely unprepared for the noise and speed of the passing cars and trucks in the misting rain. It was deafening! A vehicle passed every two seconds and the wind blasted so hard after each vehicle that I could hardly hold onto the ropes as I pulled at the tarpaulin. I turned my back to the oncoming traffic to shield myself from the wind and noise. My hands were cold and shaking as I fought with the ropes and I kept praying no one would stop. I finished one problem spot and quickly turned to run around the back of the truck to attend another.

I immediately felt an impact! As I turned I ran directly into a huge man standing not two feet behind me! I did not hear our bodies collide because of the noise around us, but I knew the sound was out there, written over us in bold red letters like in the comic books. SMACK!

Because of the traffic noise I had not heard his car pull off the road and park behind my truck. Fortunately the man was a Georgia State Trooper, but in that terrifying moment that did not register in my brain. At that moment he was just a large, strange man with an imprint of my eye makeup on his jacket.

My first reaction, as I bounced off this man's chest, was to scream like an Indian in his face while my feet did a war dance. The reaction of this man who stood in front of me was to do much the same. Obviously I had scared the daylights out of this brave trooper as well with my unexpected behavior. I was not sure who was startled more, but being a trained professional, he recovered first.

In an excited voice he yelled into the wind, "Now, calm down, Ma'am, its' okay. I'm here to help you!" And he waved both hands wildly in front of his body as he tried to defend himself from my wild trashing hands and calm me down.

At that moment he reminded me of Barney Fife trying to convince me that he carried one bad bullet, except this man was less convincing.

I gradually regained my composure and explained to the officer the problem I was having with the loose ropes and the tarpaulin covering. He was more than willing to help me, so with shaking hands we both finished tightening the ropes and securing the tarpaulin and he assisted me back inside my pick-up truck.

As I pulled away into the traffic on that cold February day, I saw the officer in my rearview mirror wiping perspiration from his face. At the same time I saw him reach into his patrol car for his radio phone. I could imagine his conversation as he reported to headquarters that he had been tying up loose ends on I-85 East with a female motorist who was loosely wrapped and in danger of losing her covering.

The Lord is with me; I will not fear; "What can man do to me?" Psalm 118:6

God intended fear as an instinct for protection rather than a debilitating reaction to paralyze or cripple. The latter is the way our enemy, Satan, the author of fear, would have us to respond to fear...to paralyze and cripple. But on the other hand, for man to recklessly throw fear aside and walk head on foolishly into danger is not utilizing God's perspective on fear either.

The Lord is with me, I will not fear. "What can man do to me?" This is certainly the answer that many of God's people have tried and found sufficient. Esther, in the Old Testament certainly tested God's sufficiency in the area of fearing man and what he could do to her. Staring rejection and possible death in the face she said, "If I perish, I perish." (Esther 4:16) She knew God desired to use her as an instrument for protecting His people so she trusted Him completely for her protection and guidance. She was never paralyzed in fear or acted in reckless abandon but allowed fear to develop faith and faith tested produces endurance (see James 1:3).

Stephen, the first Christian martyr in Acts 7, found God's word sufficient for his life. He knew that Satan, the encourager of crippling fear, could use it as a tool to cause panic and helplessness. However, Stephen, through faith and the power of God's grace, did not allow that to happen. He understood he was in a win-win situation. If he lived, God still had work for him to do, which was his delight. If he died, he knew he would go to heaven, which was where he had invested his life anyway. From that vantage point Stephen could not lose, he won either way.

David Livingstone, an explorer and missionary in South Africa, wrote, "Until I finish God's purpose for me I am immortal.

After that, it does not matter." With that perspective, it takes the edge off of fear.

Until we live daily covered in the armor of God (Ephesians 6) and the power of the Holy Spirit, we will often have difficulty with fear. We will try to fight effectively with our own human strength when Jesus in the Gospels gave His children "all authority" to stand victoriously against fear (see Luke 9:1). And the scriptures remind us, "Greater is He who is in you than he (Satan) who is in the world." (1 John 4:4)

Life is a daily classroom teaching us that the antidote for fear is faith and faith gives courage. Someone once said, "Courage is fear that has said its prayers." How is your courage today; do you need to go back to the classroom? If that is the case, don't forget your textbook, the Bible.

DAY 17

TRASH TO RICHES

My mother had come from Columbus, Mississippi to visit us in Athens and I could scarcely wait to welcome her and show her an exciting time. Of course, every woman in the state of Georgia healthy enough to breathe knew that having a good time meant a trip to Rich's Department store in downtown Atlanta.

My mom, my daughter Paige, a student at University of Georgia, and I drove over to Atlanta early in the morning and arrived about the time the stores were opening. I parked the car in a parking deck across the street from Rich's. As we walked down the sidewalk I was excitedly pointing out some of the surrounding buildings and other interesting sights to my mom. I was walking in front of Mom and Paige, of course, because I was always in a hurry. Also, the sidewalk was in a sharp downhill decline forcing us to walk quickly. I was looking back over my shoulder at the two of them talking a mile a minute as we approached a traffic light at the corner.

Suddenly, I felt my body come to a jarring halt! The lower part of my body from my waist down slammed into an immovable object causing my head and upper body to catapult forward into a dark hole. My first thought was I had been hit by a truck! But to my bewilderment, I had run blindly into a large concrete trash container at the corner of the street and flipped head first, upside down, into the container.

My legs looking like a frog doing a very bad breaststroke, I struggled wildly and with much effort finally pulled myself out of the concrete trash container and finally managed to stand upright. As I was getting my feet back under me I was jerking at my skirt, which at the time was being worn more as a scarf around my neck than a skirt around my knees. Mom and Paige were no help---they just stood in shock with their mouths open looking at me as if they had just discovered I was from Mars. Paige found her voice first and said, "Mom, you know that five pounds you lost last week? Me and half of Atlanta just found it while you were upside down in that trash can."

All of my adult life I had worked hard to portray the graceful southern lady. And now I had blown the image by standing on my head in a trash can in downtown Atlanta during rush-hour traffic.

I was prepared to be mortified and embarrassed to tears, but visualizing how disgracefully funny I looked with my legs sticking out of the trash can I began to giggle. Mom and Paige began to pull themselves out of shock and they began to giggle. The giggle progressed into a knee-slapper and finally into full gales of laughter. It was the kind of laughter that causes you to lose your breath, your speech, and your pride as we three clung to the trash-can, wrenching in laughter. We could not laugh long enough, deeply enough or loudly enough to relieve the emotion. A pack of laughing hyenas would have looked solemn compared to our performance.

In the midst of our laughter, I realized the traffic had stopped for the red light and all the waiting drivers had viewed the whole incident and were experiencing their own euphoria. One truck driver was laughing so hard I was afraid he would have a heart attack. Another businessman with a red face was pounding his steering wheel with his hands and gasping for air between laughing seizures. I was thankful the changing red light rid me of my audience who so joyfully enjoyed my performance.

It took several attempts for us to leave the comic scene and get on with our shopping trip. Each time we attempted to leave the corner we would again break into body-wrenching gales. Eventually we staggered across the street, clutching each other for support and finally managed to get into Rich's.

As we entered the store the muscles in our faces fought for composure as we struggled to keep control. After all, I kept reminding the three of us, "We are in Rich's Department Store, Y'all!" As we walked down the aisle we met a businessman coming toward us. As he neared us his gaze moved down to my feet and suddenly he had a very strange expression of his face. I followed his gaze to my feet and immediately stopped in my tracks.

I was wearing a pair of open-toed heels and evidently my toes had hit the concrete trash-can with such an impact that the blow had torn the toes out of my pantyhose. My toes had pushed through the nylons which at this point had rolled up the calves of my legs.

Convulsion best describes the scene that followed. A mannequin dressed in a spring dress was nearest me, so I grabbed the dummy and held on as my body jerked in laughter. Mom, who suffered from a slight heart condition, grabbed her chest and looked like Fred Sanford waiting for "the big one." She could stand no more, but the laughter that now hurt her body, came anyway.

Paige completely lost control and fell face forward into a table of half-priced bath linens. Muffled sobs of laughter escaped from around the hand towels and bath clothes. She lifted her tear soaked face briefly for air and her wet mascara left an exact impression of her eyes on a bath towel.

The clerk in the store would have called 911 but what would she have reported? "Three women are dying of laughter on aisle five?"

We enjoyed our shopping trip that day with all the sparkle and glitter of the beautiful merchandise. One of the highlights was lunch in the famous Magnolia Tea Room enjoying chicken salad, iced tea and lemon ice box pie. We had a grand time. However, there were numerous times while we were shopping that I glanced at Mom and Paige and saw their shoulders jerking in silent laughter and I knew they were again reliving the scene at the concrete trash can. I suspect that incident would always be the most memorable part of our trip to Atlanta's Rich's Department store.

> *"And the arrogant one will stumble and fall with no one to raise him up." Jeremiah 50:32*

> *"For the Lord will be your confidence and will keep your foot from being caught." Proverbs 3:26*

The art of "surefootedness" seems to be a thing of the past. The Native Americans and early settlers knew the value of being surefooted. Their lives many times depended upon it. Daily paths led them to uncharted territory and untested terrain that could easily cause a dangerous fall.

With today's concrete and asphalt, the world is not threatened by rocks and roots embedded in paths where there is risk to footing. The slippery rocks and embedded roots lay hidden in a new path---the pathway to the mind.

There is a rush for knowledge, much like the gold rush of 1848. The call "Thar's gold in them thar hills" has been replaced with, "thar's knowledge in them thar halls." Panning has been replaced by advanced degrees, computers, internet and numerous electronic devices.

This is definitely a move toward the betterment of all mankind, but in the search for a pathway to knowledge there has not necessarily been a search for wisdom and what is good in God's eyes.

Man has been caught up in his ability to do and know all things and as a result, he tends to become more and more smug, arrogant and self-sufficient. His reasoning is that if he learns enough and knows enough he will not need anyone other than himself. In the end he is much like the greedy old gold digger who never seemed to be satisfied with his findings; he wanted more so that his fate would be secure and in his control.

It is this path of greed and arrogance that eventually leads to the stumbling of man. His self-sufficiency will one day be challenged by the situation that is impossible for him to solve or understand despite all of his knowledge and electronic capability.

God has given man a brain and intended that he experience his full capability of learning and to glorify God with the results. But God also desires that man understand and obey Proverbs 1:7 "The fear of the Lord is the beginning of knowledge." Really? God wants us to fear Him? Someone once defined this fear by saying, "The fear of the Lord does not weaken you but strengthens you and quickens you and reflects the God within you." God desires to teach us that all we are and all we can be is a result of the great love that He has for us.

This is the knowledge that leads to wisdom which is seeing life from God's point of view. Oswald Chambers said, "If a man wants scientific knowledge, intellectual curiosity is his guide, but if he wants insight into what Jesus Christ teaches, he can only get it by obedience."*

We should give God all praise and glory for our ability to explore intellectually but above all, hold fast to the teachings of Jesus Christ. Then wherever our paths lead, God will be our confidence and will keep our foot from being caught.

*Oswald Chambers, "My Utmost for His Highest", Copyright, 1935, by Dobb, Mead & Company, Inc. Page 209.

WARNING SHOT

Bird dogs and subdivisions are always a problem. Mostly because bird dogs are continually on watch, not necessarily for birds, but for anything that moves. And of course if it moves---they bark---over and over---they bark. It does not matter that the time is high noon or midnight, if a grasshopper or clanging trash can lid gets their attention, they bark.

Mike always had four to six dogs in our pens and their value ranges from field trial winner to no good a'tall. As far as I am concerned, they are all in the latter category. However, one of his favorite dogs was a liver pointer called Tater Bug whose grandfather had been a field trial winner. "A man only gets a dog like this once in a lifetime," was a statement Mike had made so many times that I usually lip-synched the words with him. But he was so proud of Tater Bug that if she could have learned to make his favorite homemade biscuits, my position around our house would have been in jeopardy.

Nevertheless, when one of those dogs got excited and began to bark, all of them barked. Their favorite place for barking was standing on top of their doghouses. From that vantage point they could really turn their vocal cords loose. Most certainly, this made for some pretty unhappy neighbors.

Mike's method for dealing with this problem was pretty ingenious. He had an air rifle that he used to shoot carpenter bees with during the summer months and also kept him in target practice for quail season in the fall. When the dogs barked, rather than making numerous trips to the dog pens at all hours of the day or night to quiet them, he would push the gun barrel out the window in our bathroom upstairs and shoot the doghouses. The BB bouncing off the doghouse would frighten them and cause them to scamper for cover. In fact, the dogs had become so accustomed to the sound of the gun shooting that we did not even have to load the gun to stop their barking. We just cocked it, pointed the gun outside the window (through a special hole in the screen) and pulled the trigger and they would run for cover into the doghouses and hush.

One particular week Mike was out of town working and the dogs did double duty on their vocal practice. It seemed every police car and fire truck in town ran up and down our street and every cat in the neighborhood ran across our yard a dozen times during the night.

I did not pay attention to Mike the day before he left on his trip as he wiped and oiled the gun that stood safely in the locked closet in our bathroom. I did not hear all of his conversation on the phone as he told his friends about a new .22 rifle he had bought and how lightweight and easy to handle it was. It was all man talk and I had heard it a hundred times. I also did not know he stood this gun in the closet where the dog silencer (B.B. gun) stood.

That week as the dogs were responding to all the noises around them, particularly the night-prowling cats, it was impossible for me to sleep. Several nights, half-asleep, I got out of bed in the dark and went to the closet in the bathroom to find the gun. I cocked it, pointed it at the doghouses and shot. I kept thinking, "This gun shoots crisper since Mike oiled and cleaned it." The dogs certainly scampered for cover in a hurry. "Maybe they think it sounds crisper too," I thought.

At the end of the week Mike came home and we were in our bedroom unpacking his suitcase and getting caught up on the week's news. I told him the dogs had driven me crazy the first part of the week but after using the air rifle they had eventually settled down. He was walking by the closet in the bathroom as I talked and glanced to where the guns stood and he instantly froze. With eyes bulging he said, "This is not the gun you used is it?" holding up the new gun that looked very much like the old air rifle. "Yes," I said. "Sure sounds crisper since you oiled and cleaned it."

His feet never touched the stairs as he ran out of the house. He ran the 30 yards to the dog pen faster than he did in college on the football team and he now weighed 30 pounds more.

All the dogs in the pen ran to greet him with Tater Bug in the lead. They did not seem to mind the new holes in the doghouses; they just let in more air and light.

We sold that house a year later and the new owner put chickens in the dog pens. Mike saw the new owner later and asked him if the neighbors minded having chickens so close to them in the manicured, middle-class neighborhood.

"No", he said. "In fact, their comments are, "Chickens don't bark."

"And we know that God causes all things to work together for good to them who love God, to those who are called according to His purpose." Romans 8:28

Have particular circumstances in life conditioned you to flinch, duck or run and hide? Perhaps it was a traumatizing experience that left you with a memory of fear and apprehension. To another individual the same situation is not a threat, but for you there is imminent danger that is best avoided if at all possible.

There are many excellent hunting dogs that have problems of this type. One problem in particular is the possibility of becoming gun-shy. As young pups unexpected loud noises such as a thunderstorm or firecrackers exploding can frighten them so badly that they never recover and forget the fear . As a result, when they become mature dogs they miss the thing in life for which they have been created because of this frightening experience as a pup. So they live their lives in protection mode and intentionally keep themselves clear of situations that may bring back past fear.

Satan, who is a deceiver and a spoiler, will try to use painful circumstances in our lives for evil if we allow him to. He will remind us of failure, fears and disappointments to keep us from the freedom to be all that God designed for us to become. But the scripture in Romans 8:28 says that God causes all things, including the painful and disappointing experience, to work together for good to those who love Him and are called according to His purpose. Because of Jesus' perfect sacrifice on the cross, the devil has been defeated so no evil or hurtful way can abort the purpose God has for our lives...unless we, ourselves allow it. How do we allow it? By lack of faith or not understanding and using the spiritual authority that Christ's death on the cross provided for God's children.

So it is very important as believers to understand the spiritual authority Christ has given us against the devil. Because like a gun-shy dog, we too can miss the thing in life for which we were created. We could possibly be on the threshold of a wonderful opportunity from God but because we cannot get past a hurtful experience, we will not trust God to take us to new territory that He desires to give us. Rather, we fear the threat of Satan more than trust the power of God.

We need to go back to the scriptures to reclaim our spiritual weapons. Jesus tells us clearly, "In the world you have tribulation, but take courage, I have overcome the world." (John16:33) So, let us become "over-comers" and begin claiming the blood of Jesus and command the enemy to leave our lives and the plan and purpose God has for us.

Jesus also says in Luke 10:19, "I give you authority over all the power of the enemy and nothing shall injure you." So we need to speak out loud, commanding the devil that he has no right to our present or future and he cannot hold us back from all that God has for our life in JESUS NAME. It is only in the name of Jesus that we have authority over Satan.

In our walk with God, we cannot afford to become gun-shy but we can afford to trust God enough to become battle-tested. Then, the next time a situation comes along that reminds us of an old threat, don't run for cover, but run for Christ and allow God to use it for good.

DAY 19

CAPP'S STORY

"Dog is man's best friend" is one of the most exaggerated statements ever made. I have seen and owned lazy dogs, mean dogs, crazy dogs, disobedient dogs, sneaky dogs, and stupid dogs and I would not want to call any one of them my best friend.

And then there was Peppers Capperina, Capp, for short. She was intelligent, sensitive, trustworthy, loyal and completely and wholeheartedly in love with our family. We brought her fat, round body home when she was two months old and she made herself at home immediately. She did this by chewing off the leg of a fern stand and later, after the soil was well ground into the dining room carpet, she slipped upstairs to sleep under our son's bed.

All three of our children were young at this time and each fell madly in love with Capp. She returned the affection in double proportion to each one of the three.

She was with the children constantly running through the neighborhood where we lived or playing in the woods. Then later in the evening, the four of them gathered in front of the television to relax.

During the school day while the children were away she was my protector. She lay on the kitchen floor, never on the carpet, and kept me company until school was over. But the moment the school bus arrived, she ran out the door greeting each of the children and each child had their own special greeting for her as they romped across the yard.

Mike trained bird dogs as a hobby and was fairly successful with most of the techniques that he used. But he had never trained a lab. Capp was our first. However, his experience had taught him that the best training for a dog was to give it to a child and simply let the child love the dog and the dog love in return. And then, he said, if the dog is any good---teaching other things will come easily. With three children romping through our house, this certainly seemed to be the easiest method to use, so we gave it a try.

Capp was a working dog and she developed her own working relationship with each member of the family. With me she was my companion and protector. With the girls, Paige and Angie, she was gentle and patient and hid her pride as they dressed her in scarves, sweaters and old dance tutus. With our son, Kelly, she was rougher and they loved their romps in the woods and the wrestling matches in the yard.

But with Mike, she was all business. She knew he was the master of the house and when he picked up a gun to take her to hunt for duck and dove, she was devoted to him completely.

After Capp was grown and was an indispensable part of the family, we built our last home by a lake. In this house we planned to finish rearing our children and planned enough room for the grandchildren that would come in the future.

We had sold our present home and had moved into a small apartment until we completed the new house. Living in an apartment definitely cramped Capp's style so I took her to the new house site daily to exercise.

Since Mike traveled a great deal in his work I had the responsibility of checking on the house every day. This required working with the many carpenters, plumbers, brick layers, electricians and other crews. I had no idea this would be a problem for Capp until the first day on the site. Her protective instincts were so strong that each time one of the men approached me to ask questions or get instruction, she would immediately move between me and the man. Occasionally there were more men than she could shield me from safely, so she would push her seventy pounds of muscled body close to my legs and rumble a deep growl that would cause any man to whimper in retreat. However, just a few strokes from my hand and a couple of reassuring words and she would calm down.

Obviously she soon earned quite a reputation for herself among all the men working. Even though she never offered to bite anyone, the threat was there and the men were certainly aware of it.

There was one crew in particular that was respectful of Capp and I believe she was aware of their apprehension. This crew was a fun-loving group of men who were always poking fun and teasing each other and when they had nothing to laugh about, they laid bricks. One of the things they teased each other about was Capp.

One particular day I overheard one of their light-hearted conversations on this subject. I heard the foreman say to a long-legged skinny young man, "Sam, here comes that black dog you're so scared of. You better run, boy!"

Sam flinched and jerked around with his head jerking in a dozen directions at once. Then seeing no threat, relaxed and said, "I'm not afraid of that dog. I 'spect her bark is worse than her bite and I bet five minutes alone with her and I would show her who's boss."

An elderly man on the crew eye-balling his level on a row of bricks remarked, "That dog means business son, you better leave her alone. I have learned the hard way that anytime you think you have influence, try ordering another man's dog around."

A mischievous young man wearing a baseball cap with the bill pulled to the back of his head was pushing a wheelbarrow full of bricks. "Sam", he said, "you let me know when you're going to check out that dog's bark and her bite and I'll reserve me a spot in that poplar tree over there with the low limbs on it."

Then all the workers laughed and continued to brag and tease.

Late one afternoon a few days later, Mike and I drove out to check on the progress of the house. We had Capp with us of course Mike wanted to give her a workout in the lake. We assumed all the workers were gone, but unknown to us the bricking crew was working late. They had parked their pick-up trucks behind the house out of sight. They were working on the chimney at the end of the house. The back fill had not been done around the house yet so the opening on the main level for the fireplace was about eight to ten feet from the ground. The men were tired and working quietly. Mike, Capp and I, not knowing anyone was there, walked around the end of the house to see if the bricking on the chimney had begun.

Just before we rounded the corner, Capp caught scent of the men and had the advantage. As she rounded the corner, she was already an explosion of guttural growl and bark as her muscled body charged into the midst of the bewildered men.

Sam, the bragger, was nearest and when he saw Capp he looked like the coyote in a Roadrunner cartoon just before the freight train ran over him. He had a brick in one hand and a trowel loaded with cement in the other. He threw both in the air, yelled like a girl and took one step and scaled the ten-foot wall to the fireplace opening like a spider and landed in the house.

From that moment on everything was in total chaos. The men ran in all directions screaming threats and hollering at Capp. She responded with deep growls and frenzied barking as she charged each man and stopped just before actually touching him. Her large paws threw sand and gravel everywhere.

The young boy with the baseball cap on backwards was standing near his poplar tree. He did not even look at the tree; he was watching Capp and he went up the tree like he had lived in one all of his life.

A couple of other men also went through the fireplace opening, turning over wheelbarrows of mortar and brick as they ran. Another man jumped a fence to the adjoining property and the older man found safety in the bed of a pick-up truck.

Mike and I were spellbound by the circus performance before us. Eventually, Mike came out of his trance and grabbed Capp as she ran past him.

Instantly there was complete silence. You could almost hear a heartbeat. Bricks were strewn everywhere, wheelbarrows were overturned and mortar was spilling onto the ground. The only thing moving was the dust settling. The silence was almost deafening.

Very softly, the young man in the poplar tree began to snicker. The baseball cap now had the bill on the side of his head which added to the comedy of the moment. He could stand it no longer so he threw his head back and horse-laughed.

One by one the others joined in until all of us were lost in laughter. The older man in the truck bed yelled toward the house through choaking, lung- clearing laughter, "Hey Sam! You want your five minutes with that black dog now?"

Capp sat down by me panting, her pink tongue hanging out the side of her mouth drooling saliva; she looked around at each one of us. Then she licked me on the hand as if to size up the experience as all in a day's work.

> *"Unless the Lord builds the house, they labor*
> *in vain who build it." Psalm 127:1*

There is a famous children's story, The Three Little Pigs, which tells of the pigs building three different houses with different building materials. One chose to build his house of hay, the second built his house of sticks and the third built his house of brick. The villain, Big Bad Wolf, easily blows the first two houses down while the pigs watch helplessly nearby. The third wise pig built his house of more substantial, solid materials and it withstood the attack of the huffing, puffing wolf regardless of how hard he blew.

It is interesting that we see this same tragic disaster happening to homes today. From the beginning of time men have been building homes like the first two little pigs. Their homes and marriages are fragile---built with little or no solid foundation and building materials and eventually when stress and hurt comes into the marriage, it is blown apart by the villain, Satan. There is good possibility that the couple spent little to no attention to the marriage blueprints drawn by the Master Carpenter in the Bible.

Statistics show that almost half the marriages today are ending in divorce. And many couples that are staying in the covenant of marriage are filled with unhappiness and seemingly insurmountable problems that spill over onto the children. The children in turn are fearful and angry and many times live out the same mistakes in their own adult lives as the parents, so the cycle continues.

There is indication of pain and suffering in homes all across our country. The reason for this is that the evil forces of the world are centering their attack upon one of the most precious covenants to God, the marriage and family. Unlike the wolf in the fairy tale, these evil demonic forces are many times difficult to recognize. They come in the form of worldliness, lack of commitment, doing what feels good, taking the easy way out or stubborn pride.

But then there is a story in another book, the Bible, which was written long before the Three Little Pigs. It is a story told by Jesus, also about houses and building materials. One house is built on rock by the wise man, another on sand by a foolish man (see Matthew 7:24-27).

The story tells us that the house built on rock stands, despite the trials of life. The house built on sand falls when the trials and temptations of life become too strong "and great was its fall" the scripture says, because there is nothing small about a marriage and family falling apart---the repercussions are great.

To many people it may be difficult to understand why a family can be torn apart when it begins with good building materials such as love, devotion, purpose and good intentions. As worthy as these characteristics are unless the Lord is in the center of the marriage our efforts alone are in vain. Why? What we build in our strength is often too fragile to stand in this fallen world; and if it stands it is far less than what it could be with the strength and power of God.

Heartbroken men and women down through the ages have cried, "But my marriage problem was too big, too bad, too hopeless, too far gone and the devil was too ferocious! Nobody could save it." God's Word says in Psalm 147:5 and 6, "Great is our Lord, and abundant in strength; His understanding is infinite. The Lord supports the afflicted; He brings down the wicked to the ground." So according to this Scripture God has all the power we need and the devil does not stand a chance.

Perhaps you need to begin marriage renovation today on God's foundation so that your marriage is well-grounded in the scriptures. Do not labor in vain...allow God to give you quality building materials that last.

BACK OF THE WOODSHED

Back of the woodshed is a place to grow,
Learning life's lessons and painful things to know.
Both parent and child have been there,
usually when child is bad.
But who has learned the most there...
the child or Mom and Dad?

IN THE FIELD

Grandma Becky Carden was steel all the way down to her shoe-laces and her reputation was known throughout the Coal Fire, Alabama area. She was a woman of the 30s, 40s, and 50s, living through the Great Depression, several wars and rearing five children of her own and several orphans. All this she did and make ends meet on an 80-acre farm that she and her husband, John B. farmed.

Becky was a woman gifted in many areas. She was known throughout the area as a mid-wife and was called on many days and nights to bring a new life into the world. She was also called upon as a physician and she came with her kerosene to pour on snake- bites and salves to rub on wounds resulting from farming accidents. She was sought out as a counselor in family and marriage disputes. Many a time she would shake her finger in a feuding couple's faces and give them a lecture somewhere between a sermon and a cussing out. It seemed to be just what the couple needed to give them a new perspective on their problems and they would vow to try harder to work things out.

Grandpa Carden had been a school teacher before marrying Grandma Becky, who was his pupil. He was a genteel man, small in stature and he worked hard raising cotton on their farm.

It is not fair to say Grandpa raised the crop all by himself. He had the help of one lone white mule…Sam.

Sam was like most mules, only more so. He was a stubborn, independent and unmotivated animal who frequently balked in the middle of a cotton row and refused to move. His marble-sized brain was capable of recording only one piece of information and he hit pay dirt with his selection in regard to Grandpa. He knew Grandpa had rather be sitting on the back porch listening to Dizzy Dean broadcast a St. Louis Cardinal Baseball game on the radio than walking behind a plow with a boring view of a mule's posterior. Instinctively he knew the longer it took for them to finish the plowing the later Grandpa was for his ballgame…so consequently, there was always a battle raging between the two.

Grandpa was always screaming and jerking plow lines while Sam balked and stood cool and unconcerned in the cotton rows. If an observer were asked who represented the authority figure of the two, Sam would have won hands down.

On a hot summer day, Grandma was working in her kitchen when she heard Grandpa's voice yelling for her from the nearby field. Grandma knew something was terribly wrong so she hurried out of the house and headed for the field as fast as she could run. Finally reaching the hot dusty rows where Grandpa was plowing, Becky's eyes searched Grandpa for signs of physical harm. But it did not take her long to see Grandpa's injury was not physical but emotional and he was like a volcano ready to explode.

Anger is a terrible thing…especially when an animal with an IQ of about fifteen infuses the anger into a man with perfectly good sense. Sam had sat down in the middle of a cotton row and refused to move. Grandpa knew his ballgame was probably well on its way and if he did not hurry he would miss it altogether.

He was so enraged he was picking up dirt with his bare hands and throwing it on Sam. This did not relieve his boiling frustration so he began kicking the dirt on Sam with his feet. Then he stopped long enough to use his straw hat to beat Sam around the head and ears. He was sweating and foaming around the mouth and telling the good Lord that He may have made one mistake and that was creating this animal. Sam continued to sit on his back haunches, ears flopped back, eyes staring straight ahead and acting unconcerned with the whole matter.

Grandma quickly appraised the situation and realized that if she did not do something quickly Grandpa could have a stroke. She shouted firmly, "John B, put yor' hat on yor' head and get behind that plow and take a hold of them reins." She then walked around to Sam's head and grabbed a hold of his ear. She folded it over like a thick slice of sour dough bread and bit into it as if she were biting into a ham sandwich.

Pain hit Sam's pea brain and he gave a startled "heee haww" loud enough to wake the dead. He then jumped to his all fours and lunged forward, knocking Grandma backwards. She tripped and staggered but regained her balance in time to see Sam stabbing his clumsy hooves into the soil as he strained forward like he was running in a mules' version of the Kentucky Derby. Grandpa was hanging onto the plow for dear life, stumbling wildly behind the wave of fresh dirt with his feet hitting the ground only occasionally. In the distance Sam could be seen shaking his head and flicking his ear erratically trying to relieve the pain Grandma had inflicted. Grandma moved to the end of the row and stood with her hands on her hips and a grin on her face as she spit gray mule hair from her mouth.

Grandpa finished his plowing that day and put Sam in the barn. He went to the house and sat down on the back porch. Grandma gave him a big glass of cold water and then switched on the radio just in time for him to hear Dizzy say the afternoon game was in the bottom of the ninth, two outs, no runners on base and the Cardinals were leading 3 to 1.

Grandpa released a long deep sign and leaned his straight-back chair against the wall of the cool porch to get more comfortable. His beloved Cardinals were in the field and winning. But his satisfaction at the moment was not coming completely from the ballgame. His satisfaction was also in knowing that Sam was in the barn with a sore ear and a deflated mule ego. Grandpa took the liberty of believing that even that crazy ole pea brain mule knew that he, John B. Carden, had won in the field that day... with the help of Grandma Becky Carden of course.

> *In all your ways acknowledge Him and He will make your paths straight. Proverbs 3:6*

> *Commit your work to the Lord, and your plans will be established. Proverbs 16:3*

Frustration in career roles in the marketplace has been experienced since man left the Garden of Eden and entered the fallen world to earn a living for his family. It has been felt by the farmer in the hot, dusty fields to the businessmen and women in a Wall Street office.

Today in our high-tech competitive work force, the pressure and stress to perform is tremendous and the results reveal that the body is taking a beating mentally, physically and emotionally. God intended that work challenge men and women but the results today seem to be the very detriment of our very lives. Our work, that should give us a sense of accomplishment and identity, is coming at a heavy price as our bodies are falling apart while scripture says our bodies are God's temple to reflect His glory.

Physicians' reports show endless cases of ulcers and stomach disorders. Millions suffer from insomnia and similar numbers are victims of stroke, heart attack, and even cancer as a result of stress and overwork. It also cannot go unnoticed the countless number of families that suffer from divorce and broken relationships as a result of frustration from work and career responsibilities.

Proverbs 16:3 tells us that God never intended for us to show up alone for work. God is the equipper for every area of our lives through the power of His Word and the presence of the Holy Spirit. Proverbs 3:6 says, "In all your ways acknowledge Him and He will make your paths straight." This explains why many times our lives (paths) become tangled with added problems of poor health and poor business judgment because we are not allowing God to have control in these areas of our lives. The scripture says, "In *all* your ways", that should cover the work hours as well.

Perhaps we hesitate to give God control in our career because we doubt His business sense. Sure, He can make rain and hold the earth in orbit, but can He understand the complexity of the electronic age and does He grasp the intensity of the world market of production and sales?

The answer is yes, God understands the electronic age. In fact, He made the first computer then placed it in Adam's head and called it a brain. Yes, He can grasp the intensity of production and sales. In the book of Exodus He so guided the life of young Joseph in the knowledge of production and sales that Joseph understood how to grow enough grain to fill storehouses to feed several million people for seven years. Then God made Joseph the general manager of Egypt. That is a great example of climbing the corporate ladder. Joseph was able to do all of this without a stroke or heart attack. God simply "established his plans."

God's desire is that His people live with peace of mind as well as physical, emotional, and financial prosperity as we walk in our paths in this fallen world. And when we demonstrate this Christ like countenance in our careers it is a dynamic way to reveal the power of our God and the authority He gives His children to lay claim to all He has for them. A powerful scripture in 2 Chronicles 16:9 says "For the eyes of the Lord move to and fro throughout the earth that He may strongly support those whose heart is completely His." When we give our heart to Him "completely," which includes our career, then according to the scriptures, we have His strong support. Sounds like a sure way to find a straight path to success.

MODEL T

My mother's dad was a quiet, tenderhearted man who rarely raised his voice. John B. Carden did not have to raise his voice. He left the yelling to his wife, Becky. He taught school several years before Becky came into his classroom and stole his heart and they were married a while later. Being a disciplinarian to a room filled with rowdy Alabama farm kids did not come naturally for John B., so he left the teaching profession and became a farmer.

John B. and Becky had five children, three boys and two girls, and they raised them on the farm along with cotton, corn, summer vegetables, cows, chickens and a pig or two. My mother, Jessie Lee, was the youngest of the five children and unlike her older sister, Viola, she was a daring, mischievous, carefree tomboy.

The three boys were named Milton, Edward and Eunice. Typical of southerners Grandma Becky was one for double names for her children so she taught the children to call the boys Brother Eunice, Brother Edward and Brother Milton.

However, as young children will do, they had their own way of pronouncing the boy's names and Brother became Bubba and eventually Bubba became Ba. So the Carden boys were called

BaEd, BaEune, and because Milton always had an attitude, they called him BaButt. These names stuck on the boys and they were called this all their lives by friends and family alike. It was interesting that when these men eventually left home BaEune became an officer and career man in the U.S. Army. BaEd established a million dollar baking business in Detroit and BaButt became an executive in an insurance company in Nashville. No matter, when they came back to Coal Fire, Alabama they were still BaEd, BaEune, and BaButt.

John B., who never owned a tractor to help with the farming of his land, was one of the first men in Pickens County to own a Model T. Ford. In the year 1916 half of the cars sold in America were Fords and Henry Ford sold the Model T's for $400.00 a car.

John B. bought his Ford the summer of 1920 and parked it in the back yard for everyone to admire. All five children took their turn sitting behind the steering wheel and turning all the levers and pushing all the buttons. They wallowed it to death and rubbed it raw as they examined it from one end to the other. Never had they seen anything so grand and the children could not wait their turn to take a ride.

Eventually the three older children, BaEd, BaButt and Viola, had seen enough and they drifted back inside the house out of the heat.

The adventuresome nature and curiosity of BaEune and Jessie Lee was not yet satisfied and after everyone left them alone, they decide to take this new toy apart and see how it worked. It was hard for them to take this piece of technology seriously. If it did not swish flies with its tail or chew its cud, it was a toy as far as they were concerned and toys were made to be played with.

So piece by piece they began to dismantle the beautiful car. They removed the fenders, running board, tires and were working on more serious parts when Viola came out of the house and stepped onto the porch, slamming the screen door behind her. She walked to the end of the porch to the well bucket and was half way through a dipper of water when she saw what was happening.

She saw the pieces of the car strewn all over the yard and her mouth fell open in shock. BaEune and Jessie Lee, with sweat running off their grease smeared faces were as busy as two bees.

Instinctively Viola assumed her older sister stance which was smacking both hands on her hips and hollering loudly, "Papa's going to wear you two out when he sees what y'all done!" Her red curls bounced as she spit out each word.

BaEune, unscrewing the bolts on the right front door said, "We're not afraid of Papa, are we, Doodle?" (Jessie Lee's nickname). Slowly a cockly little grin spread over his handsome, adolescent face and he snapped a wicked wink in Doodle's direction. "Nope," said Doodle as a mirror fell off the car into her hands.

Viola, ("Sister" was her nickname) turned on her bare heel and ran back into the house, slamming the screen door again, and did what older sisters do...she told on 'em.

John B. was completely relaxed and listening to a baseball game on the radio. He was in his favorite rocker with his bare feet propped up, drinking a cool glass of buttermilk. When Viola relayed her information to him in her tattletale voice, he spewed buttermilk all over the radio and hit the floor running.

BaEune was leaning a car door against the smoke house when John B. threw open the screen door on the run.

BaEune had never seen Papa mad. In fact it was usually his Mom who took a limb to him so he had never really tested Papa's disciplinary tactics and this did not look like a good time to start. Throwing his tools behind him BaEune bolted across the yard toward the pasture with Papa in hot pursuit. Both of them barefooted, side-stepped cow patties as they ran as hard as they could run.

Everyone in the house was now standing on the porch watching the two disappear into the woods on the far side of the pasture. Viola, having completed her mission, was standing with her hands still on her hips. BaEd had an impish grin on his face, secretly hoping BaEune could keep the lead. And BaButt was saying he hoped Papa did not forget about Doodle, who he could see hiding under the smoke house. Everyone began to find a seat on the porch to get comfortable and wait to see how the drama was going to play out. All eyes were scanning eastward, toward the woods where Papa and BaEune had disappeared.

An hour crept by and Becky began to grow uneasy. She had seen John B.'s temper tested on a few occasions and she knew he did not handle it well. For a quite mannered man it took a lot to make him lose his composure; but when he lost it everyone knew to back away. So son or not, she wasn't sure how he would deal with BaEune.

While everyone was waiting to see what was going to happen, Becky slipped out of the house and hurried into the woods in the general direction where she last saw John B. and BaEune running. She pushed her way through the woods, stopping occasionally to listen in case she might hear BaEune begging his Papa for mercy. Eventually she heard voices and she crept toward them, being careful to stay hidden.

Sitting on a log near the creek in the thick woods filled with muscadine and honeysuckle vines were John B. and BaEune. Both father and son were completely and totally exhausted from running and dodging all the underbrush in the woods. They had run until they could run no longer. There was no energy left to give a whipping or resist a whipping so they both gave up and sat down on the log. Neither was aware of Becky hiding in the bushes near them.

Finally John B., gasping for breath, said to BaEune, "Son, do you think you can put that car back together?" BaEune, with sweaty hair standing in spikes on his head, looked at his papa and in a scared, weak voice said, "Yep, Papa, I reckon I can." His lips trembled and tears ran through car grease on his face.

John B. wanted desperately to rub his bleeding feet but knew he had not missed all the cow patties so he decided not too. "BaEune, when we get back to the house, and you're asked what happened between the two of us, will you promise to tell everybody that I beat the tar out of you with a stick?" He paused a moment to get his breath and continued, "If you can promise me that, well son, when we're able we'll get up and walk out of here."

BaEune, relief in his tear-filled eyes said, "That's fine with me Papa. I reckon you don't have to whup me anyway, you done scart' the daylights out of me."

Becky, still listening in the bushes, was resisting a strong urge to get a big stick and beat them both. But, with a smile on her lips, she eased out of the wild huckleberry bushes and headed back to the house.

Yet those who wait for the Lord will gain new strength. They will mount up with wings like eagles. They will run and not get tired, they will walk and not become weary. Isaiah 40:31

The medical profession spends a great deal of time taking care of illnesses related to fatigue. The public seems more and more susceptible to physical problems that are a result of overwork, stress and exhaustion. And no wonder…society is frantically trying to work into its schedules fulltime occupation, family time, play time, individual time and all of the unexpected things that eat up time. Eventually the body begins to wear out physically, mentally, emotionally and spiritually.

Isaiah 40:31 has a wonderful prescription for those who have this problem. The key word in this prescription is 'wait.' But in our busy society that moves faster than the speed of sound, the word 'wait' is an unpleasant word. No one has time to wait! So like naughty children responding to the unpleasant taste of a healing medication, we push away that which will cure us and choose not to take it at all.

But God says if we wait upon Him and gain His perspective on a healthy schedule, that by His healing, energizing Word, He will give us new strength. This will not be just strength to drag through a day, but we will be able to soar above the mundane as if we had wings of eagles. What a way to live and what a perspective. As we pray to the Father, pray this verse out loud speaking our names into the verse and apply it to our lives personally. God in heaven is waiting to answer and give us renewed life each day.

David, the Psalmist, knew of the importance of this 'wait'. He says in Psalms 25:5, "Lead me in Thy truth and teach me, For Thou art the God my salvation; For thee I wait all the day." We should take David's advice and slow down and listen for God to speak and refresh.

Obviously life has a way of wearing us down and wearing us out. But when we refuel with the scripture, we can run and not get tired, we will walk and not become weary.

Do you need a second wind? Take a daily dose of God's prescription...wait upon the Lord.

A CHICKEN IN EVERY POT

My Dad was a great storyteller. He just naturally had a way with words. He dropped out of school after the third grade, but that did not seem to limit his ability to communicate effectively, especially when telling a yarn.

Dad's best stories were about himself and he could get into some real predicaments so he had a wealth of resource material. He could also see the humor in a situation no matter how bad the circumstances and he was never too proud to tell a story even if he was the brunt of the joke.

As a girl I remember some of his favorite stories were about the economic depression in the late thirties and early forties. It sounded like the most horrible time in the world to me. But when Daddy told his stories, which always started off so grave and somber, he finished them with everyone getting their best laugh of the day.

Mom and Dad married in 1930 and soon afterwards the effects of the depression began to be felt by our country. There was no work to be found for thousands of people and Dad was one of the thousands.

During this time Mom and Dad's first child, John Wyman, was born. As delighted as they were with their new son, it certainly added to Dad's anxiety.

They moved to Canton, Mississippi right after John Wyman was born. Dad had an uncle and aunt, Boyd and Sadie McCoy, who owned a saw mill there and they wrote to Dad that they had some work for him. Uncle Boyd gave him fifty cents a day and a one-room house on the back of the property for Dad and his family to live in. It was not much but it was enough for the time being.

Dad's success was short-lived however, because soon after he and Mom settled in he was laid off and the mill closed.

Dad joined the many other people in town looking for work everyday and standing in the soup line for a free meal. After each exasperating day he would walk back to the small house where Mom waited anxiously hoping that he would have good news when he arrived.

After many days of unrewarded efforts, Dad arrived home desperate and at his wits end. He sat in the little room by the open door to think through their situation as he had done every afternoon. He wondered how they were going to live for the next few days.

They were living from meal to meal and at the moment there was nothing for them to eat for supper. He sat forward in his chair with his elbows on his knees and his head in his hands. Life never looked so unkind.

Most unexpectedly through the open door walked a free-range Rhode-Island Red chicken. She walked across the threshold and into the room as if she had done it every day of her life. Dad lifted his head out of his hands and looked at the chicken like it was the first time he had ever seen one. There was a long, still silence and in that silence Dad suddenly saw supper on the table. The only thought going through his mind at the moment was, "Come on in chicken, come on in." And at the same time was thinking what a Rhode-Island chicken taste like.

The chicken walked a couple more steps into the room and stopped, poised on one leg, cocked her head to one side and froze. Dad was also frozen, but slowly lifted his leg and gently pushed the door shut with his foot.

He looked at Mom and said, "If the good Lord had not wanted us to have this chicken for supper, He would not have let her come through the door."

There was a mess of feathers to clean up in that little house later but the chicken fed them until Dad's next job.

"And my God shall supply all your needs according to His riches in glory in Christ Jesus." Philippians 4:19

"Boy, are you lucky," is an ageless remark used by most everybody at one time or another. A noticeable blessing comes into our lives and it is immediately attributed to luck.

On a daily basis our lives are filled with events that cause us to shake our heads in wonder at how misfortune or tragedy passed us by. A near miss on the highway that could have been fatal, a critically ill child that suddenly got better or a stretched budget that somehow stretched far enough for school tuition. All of these blessings would get a "Boy are you lucky," from those watching.

It must be disturbing to our Heavenly Father to see that His children are more likely to believe that some fat genie has tossed the die rather than the almighty hand of God, Jehovah Jireh, provided a need.

God many times is robbed of the glory and praise He should receive after faithfully answering those panicked prayers that are quickly whispered to Him in the quietness of a troubled heart. He is robbed because His children later brush it off as luck or coincidence or too embarrassed to say openly, "Praise God" or "Thank you Father!"

God has promised to supply all our needs. Matthew 6:8 says, "...your Father knows what you need, before you ask Him." He does not go to sleep or get distracted and forget to be aware of every detail of our lives. His way of providing may sometimes be surprising and His timing most unique but He tends to our needs when we ask. But I wonder how much more abundantly He would bless if we would confess to those around us that we have been claiming the promises of God in His Word rather than counting four-leaf clovers when our needs are provided.

God's delight is to provide for His children's needs; and how delighted and generous He is when we can "be anxious for nothing, but in everything by prayer and supplication with thanksgiving let your request be made known to God." (Philippians 4:6)

The next time we see a prayer answered and a need provided, we should thank God and say to those observing, "Boy, am I blessed," rather than, "Boy, am I lucky."

DAD HUNG THE MOON

Dad, commonly known to friends and family as Mac, was one of those Walter Brennan-type characters that brought a smile to everyone's face. His outgoing, fun-loving personality never met a stranger and he could strike up a conversation immediately with almost anyone around him.

As children, my brother, Herbert, and I would accompany Dad on routine errands around town. We knew how much Dad loved to talk to anyone and everyone that he ran into. So going to the store to buy a bag of flour could be a half-day trip and a fun adventure for us children. Regardless of what we were doing we dropped it and jumped into the back seat of the car, ready for the excursion. To make the event more interesting my brother and I would make a game of counting the number of conversations Dad would have from the time he left the car until he returned. We followed behind him into the store and each time he engaged someone in conversation we would stand just out of his sight, roll our eyes back in our head and hold up fingers for the number of conversations he had from the car through the store. Usually the tally would run up to a double fist-full of fingers.

Dad's favorite forms of recreation were coon hunting, raising and training coon dogs, and his favorite of all...telling coon-hunting tales. I well remember our back yard being a maze of dog houses, stakes, chains, and coon dogs occupying their circumference of space. However, there was a space in the yard just before reaching the dog territory that was known as Momma's territory. This space was defined by a wire strung between two posts and was known as Momma's clothesline. We all had learned to be careful and duck just before we reached the dogs or we could literally lose our heads.

Having all of these animals in a small urban neighborhood was always touch-and-go at the very best, but especially on a night of a full moon. Dad owned one old, scarred and chewed-up redbone hound named Red. Red had two things in common with Dad… he loved coon hunting and he loved to take advantage of a full moon to reminisce over past hunts. Of course being a dog, he reminisced by howling to the moon.

One night in particular, ole Red was exercising his vocal cords to their finest tenor under the light of an Alabama moon. His howl would begin low in his throat, then as he lifted his nose toward the moon, his bay would crescendo into chords that would raise the hair on the back of your neck.

This went on until the wee hours of the morning and finally Dad and the neighbors could stand it no longer.

Dad, one hundred and ten percent aggravated, finally decided he would have a talk with Red. These talks usually consisted of Dad grabbing Red by the loose skin on the back of his neck, jerking his head back until his eyes were pulled back on each side of his face so tight that he looked like a Pekingese. Then Dad would say between barred lips and clenched teeth, "Are you going to shut up Red? Huh? Huh?" and then he would glare at Red as if he thought the dog was going to answer him.

Dad got out of bed and tiptoed through the house in longhandle underwear and bare feet. He went out the back screen door and before it had slammed behind him he was spouting all kinds of threats to Red, getting him warmed up for the real punishment ahead.

Herbert and I had been awake all through Red's serenade and we heard Dad on the move. We jumped out of our beds, stumbled in the dark over whatever was in our path and made our way to the moonlit window just as Dad approached the clothesline. Walking gingerly on bare feet and spouting a truckload of promising threats toward Red, he clearly had revenge on his mind and a belt in his hand and Herbert and I flinched at the thought of what was ahead for the dog.

Suddenly, Dad's forward advance was interrupted and we heard a threatening sentence cut short, saw two bare feet shoot into the air and heard a body hit the ground with a thud. There on the ground lay Dad in moonlight splendor. For the first time I could ever remember, Dad lay silently. He hit the ground so hard that the wind was knocked out of him and he was gasping for air and could not even whisper a word. With so many extemporaneous threats for Red a few moments earlier, now he had nothing to say. From our window we could see it was not Red that was taking a beating from being too noisy. He had abandoned his late night performance and dived into the safety of his doghouse.

It appeared that Mom's clothesline had hung Dad out to dry and his fallen, oxygen depleted body was silent proof.

*"But Joshua commanded the people saying, You
shall not shout nor let your voice be heard, nor let a
word proceed out of your mouth until the day I tell
you, Shout, then you shall shout." Joshua 6:10*

There are times in our lives when God tells us through the
indwelling of the Holy Spirit to be quiet and listen; and then
there are other times when he prompts us to speak and to speak
confidently. It is most important to know which we should be
doing and Joshua gives us a good example of this point.

In Joshua 6:10 God is giving His people instructions through
His leader, Joshua, about how to tear down a wall around the
city of Canaan. This is a literal wall that has been constructed
from years of battle debris, stone and structured fortification
made to protect this ancient, wicked city. However, this wall
and the city within are in the path of the territory God has
planned for His children to occupy. God's battle plan according
to the scriptures instructs the Israelites to first walk around
the wall without making a sound, not uttering a word...all
three million of the people. And the Israelites are to walk this
marathon around the wall each day for seven days.

This seems to be a strange way to tear down a wall and it is not
likely that today's highly technical military strategist would see
the strength of this battle plan. But nothing is impossible for
God and His heart's desire is to show us His miraculous works
even though it may look strange at the time. And usually His
miracles only appear when there is no other possible way except
the supernatural power of God.

God's Word is relevant for every generation and when we
examine our lives today we may be more like the Israelites than

we think. Life's journey is one wall after another that stands in our path and blocks us from God's best for us. The enemy, Satan, will make sure the walls are before us by throwing one problem after another into our lives. Perhaps not literal stone walls, but emotional, mental, spiritual or circumstantial walls that block us from the territory God has for us. More specifically, when we examine our lives we may find walls that result from fear, rebellion, rejection, insecurity, disappointment, lack of forgiveness or defeat and the list can go on and on. In these cases God would give us the same instructions that He gave Joshua and the Israelites, "You shall not shout nor let your voice be heard, nor any word proceed out of your mouth until the day I tell you."

But how does this command look in our lives today? God's battle plan will tell us to step out on to our spiritual path by quietly and tenaciously studying and meditating on His Word. He would train us by giving us opportunity to press in hard and examine the scripture in our minds and allow them to drop into our hearts. The battle plan would also include spending time before the Father in prayer and allowing the Holy Spirit to minister to us and break up the areas that have become hard as stone. Then when we become *strong in the Lord and the strength of His might* (see Ephesians 6:10) ...then it is time to "Shout!" Shout our testimony to those around us about what God has done in our lives. Take authority and command the devil to leave our mind and emotions in the name of Jesus so that we can occupy the land of healthy physical, mental, spiritual and financial living. God's desire is that we become whole, nothing lacking...nothing lost, and when we follow Him and His plan, He tears down the walls that hold us back from the territory He has given us.

God trains us for endurance and confidence and the results of the training will be that we will have something of value to say to the world around us. Hebrews 10:35 and 36 says, "Therefore do not throw away your confidence, which has great reward. For you have need of endurance, so that when you have done the will of God, you may receive what was promised." We can speak with authority and confidence breaking down the walls that threaten our lives from all that God has for us. So let us ask ourselves, are we spending time walking silently...getting ready to shout?

FOUL DRIVING

If Norman Rockwell had painted a portrait of the model grandfather, Mike's granddad, Mr. Al, could have been his subject. He was every boy's dream of the perfect grandfather and Mike was the son he never had. Their physical appearance and personalities were almost identical.

Mr. Al owned a farm in north Alabama near a town called Centre and most everyone in the area knew and respected him. Not only was he grassroots America, model citizen, he was also a fine sportsman and the best shot in the whole country, so it was told. He had a big heart for people and it carried over to the creatures of the wild. He understood the value of being a good wildlife conservationist and always left grain around the edge of the field for the wildlife when he harvested his crops.

One rainy, fall Saturday before noon, Granddad, 12- year-old Mike, and Mike's Dad, George, decided to drive over to the country store. This was a man's thing to do in rural Alabama. It was an excuse to rub shoulders with the other men in the community and exchange local gossip and farm updates. Without fail, at some point during a day, there would be an overpowering urge to have a Coke and there was always one in the iced Coke box that had their name on it.

It was still raining when they left the farm in Granddad's 1951 Plymouth that Mike was allowed to drive when his dad was not around. Mike climbed into the back seat and the two men sat in front with Granddad driving. Mike enjoyed these drives because the things a boy learned listening to these two men in the front seat could not be learned in his sixth grade class. The car was filled with the smell of Granddad's pipe and dust from the surrounding fields.

They drove down the road at Granddad's favorite speed, 35 miles an hour. As they rode, they discussed the field on the right side of the road and the farm on the left side as their car passed through the misty rain.

It should be understood, that as well-respected as he was, Granddad was not a perfect man. His character was flawed by a few weaknesses and one of them was dove shooting. Now dove shooting is no crime. It's great sport---unless you shoot the dove off of power lines.

Granddad could not tolerate seeing a dove perched brazenly on a power line during dove season. Maybe he could tolerate four or five but fifteen or twenty and he would succumb to temptation and pull out a shotgun every time.

They were about halfway to the store when Granddad suddenly sat forward in his seat, pushing his large chest and stomach against the steering wheel. He glared out the windshield and saw the power line thick with doves. They were lined up like a shooting gallery in a carnival booth.

"Look a there, George, There must be fifty dove on that line!" He snapped a glance in Mike's direction in the back seat and said, "Hand me that shotgun, son, and a couple of shells." Mike grabbed the gun and shells and passed them to the front seat to his Granddad.

Granddad glanced at George and said, "Hold the wheel George and drive," as he slowed down. George knew better than argue, it would do no good. Granddad was like a thirsty longhorn that smelled water, and the pond was in sight.

He shoved the barrel of the shotgun out the window and quickly loaded two shells. Then he took slow aim at the birds.

Granddad carefully eyeballed the birds, Mike eyeballed the birds and unfortunately, George eyeballed the birds and forgot about steering the car.

About the time Granddad pulled aim the car hit a ditch and the gun fired just as they landed in three feet of water. Mike landed in the floor of the big Plymouth but was up again in time to see all of the doves flying safely away without losing a feather.

The three climbed out of the car and stood around in the mud watching the left rear tire as it revolved in midair. An approaching pick-up saw the mishap and pulled over onto the shoulder of the road. The truck was driven by a neighboring farmer, Gramlin, who was also a son-in-law of Mr. Al's.

Gramlin had a sly grin on his face as he slowly stepped out of the pick-up. He pushed his hands deep into his overalls as he walked across the muddy field toward the ditched trio. He knew Mr. Al had been overcome by temptation as he had a few times before. He stopped a few feet from the men and pushed the bill of his cap toward the back of his head. With a toothy grin on his face he said, "Dove shooting kinda rough on the Plymouth, ain't it Mr. Al?"

Granddad, knowing he was caught and guilty, also caught Mike and George grinning at him as well. Gramlin continued to enjoy having the upper hand in the situation which did not happen often with his father-in-law. He spit a spew of tobacco juice into the mud and added, "Most folks use an ole dog to get their shot dove out of the field."

Mike, enjoying the event more than Christmas, spit saliva into the mud just for practice, and thought to himself, "Yep, this is sure better than sixth grade."

And a highway will be there, a roadway, and it will
be called the Highway of Holiness. Isaiah 35:8

Living in a time of fast travel, the super expressway has become something of the norm for most cities of good size. Many highways looking much like a spaghetti junction with a maze of twisted highways and over passes, display huge cloverleaves that empty into six lanes of speeding cars and trucks. Even the experienced traveler has at times found his heart in his mouth as he makes quick decisions on which lane of asphalt is the correct one to follow.

This can be very much the way of living our daily lives for the individual unless he has made a daily study of God's road map. Life can become very twisted with unknown circumstances waiting around the curve that can lift us high in excitement or send us unexpectedly crashing to the ground. There are also many wide lanes in life lying before us that seem exciting and right to take, but after traveling on them for a while we find they lead in directions we wish we had not taken.

So how can we know how to direct our paths and read traffic signs in life…to yield, to stop, to enter, to exit, to proceed with caution or to accelerate when given the right of way?

Interestingly, the Bible is very familiar with highways and God speaks through the prophet Isaiah, "And a highway will be there, a roadway, and it will be called the Highway of Holiness." A life traveler would ask, "Where do we get on this Highway of Holiness?" Scripture will show us that it begins in a state called Kingdom Living that is referred to in Matthew 6:10 and reads, "Thy kingdom come, Thy will be done, on earth as it is in heaven." So how do we connect to this highway (as we get ready to set our GPS)? We connect when we desire to live here on earth, in the present, as it is in heaven. So it is through Kingdom Living that we will find the answers to all the questions we have about our road map of life.

But is this Highway of Holiness like a toll road and a travler has to pay to enter onto it? Isaiah continues to tell us how to enter in verse 10, "But the *redeemed* will walk there." The redeemed are those that have trusted in Jesus Christ as their Savior and not only have they trusted Him as their savior, but they have taken on His identity...which is holy.

Many may think this Highway of Holiness is boring, always telling us where we cannot go and giving warnings that always end with…STOP! But this is not always the case. This highway has many exciting trips directing us into journeys that we cannot imagine we can take and enjoy. Trips we never dreamed possible will be provided by the creator of the universe. These journeys will take us to the mountain tops, down into the valleys, and by streams of living water. There will be roads in the desert and roads by plush oasis. There will be wide roads and narrow roads and roads less traveled. And here is the most wonderful part... this journey and these roads will one day lead us to streets of gold. So may I point out---the creator is quite a travel agent as well!

A HOLE LOT OF PATIENCE

"It's a boy!" Those are the enchanted words that move a father to tears and cause his heart to explode with happiness. For a man the birth of a son gives pride to the present and hope for the future. As he gazes at the wrinkled little body that has grown from his seed, the possibilities and potential seem endless.

However, it is during that exhilarating moment of birth that the father loses his perspective and has no concept of what he will be required to endure emotionally, mentally and physically to nurture his son through the present and into the future.

Mike's plan for rearing our son was simple. He looked into the innocent face of our bundle of joy and said, "Son, always listen to my advice and follow my instructions and you will never go wrong." Mike received this revelation of child-rearing wisdom about 30 minutes after our son was born, so he was still light-headed and giddy with delusion and probably had been sniffing too many fumes from my pain medication.

But in that moment he truly thought this philosophy would work...at all times, in every situation and without frustration.

After many young years of having ample opportunity to follow this advice, our son Kelly would not always agree with the merits of this plan and though his Dad would not admit it... neither would he. Needless to say, there were many times of frustration on behalf of both father and son as one grew up and the other grew older.

Since Mike had the patience of an African warthog, he usually ended up in a rage resembling that of a wildebeest standing in a bed of fire ants. To say he suffered the most of the two emotionally is an understatement. There were many times that manhood for Kelly seemed an eternity away.

On a Saturday morning, Mike and eleven-year-old Kelly were having one of their "Always follow my instructions and you will never go wrong" discussions while Mike worked on a problem with his bass boat.

The boat was a 16-foot Allison Craft fiberglass with a 150 horsepower Mercury motor. Mike knew what was wrong with the boat but with a lack of technical vocabulary, he explained that the gizmo that helped stabilize the motor while the boat was in tow to and from the lake had cracked.

Each time Mike lowered the motor to prepare it for road travel, a lever that braced the motor by inserting into the cracked gizmo would not align and it would hit against the outside of the boat. The danger in this was that if not aligned properly, it would push a hole through the boat.

Mike instructed Kelly to stand by the motor at the end of the boat and help him. The boat was on the trailer so Mike stood on the outside where he could reach the trim tab of the throttle.

"Now Kelly," his dad said, "I'me going to lower the motor until you see the lever go into the hole. When you see the lever go into the hole, yell for me to stop."

Kelly, who was more interested in grasshoppers and squirrels jumping around the yard replied, "Okay Dad, sure," as he dropped a lizard into the live-well.

Mike began to lower the motor, lower, lower, lower. Finally, he said, "Kelly is the lever in the hole yet?"

"Uh, yeah, Dad, it's in the hole."

Mike came around to the end of the boat to check on the progress and to his horror the lever had not gone into the correct position but had pushed a hole all the way through the fiberglass boat.

Mike's mouth dropped open and he stared in disbelief at the hole in his boat! He could not believe Kelly had watched the lever punch another hole alongside the cracked gizmo. In a heartbeat he was so angry he moved right on past the wildebeest in the fire ant bed phase to a gorilla needing a root canal. He jerked his cap off his head and threw it onto the ground then kicked it into the air. Needing something more solid to get a hold of, he turned to the boat and kicked the tire on the trailer so hard it almost went flat. Pain shot up his leg and as he jerked forward to rub his foot, he slammed his head on the edge of the boat. It sounded like a coconut falling from a tree and hitting the ground with a loud thump. Forgetting his foot, he clamped his hands on each side of his head to keep the pain from exploding it all over the yard.

When the pain subsided enough for him to talk, he spit words out between clenched teeth and the saliva foaming in the corners of his mouth, "Kelly, I told you to tell me when the lever went into the hole." He tried to talk in a low calm voice, but his blood pressure was ringing in his ears so loud he had to yell to hear himself above the noise.

Kelly, who was now giving his dad his full attention answered, "I did, Dad. But you didn't tell me which hole."

> *"Behold children are a gift of the Lord; the fruit of the womb is a reward. Like arrows in the hand of a warrior, so are the children of one's youth. How blessed is the man whose quiver if full of them."*
> **Psalm 127:3-5**

Has someone ever given you what you assumed was a very precious gift and when you opened it you were sure you had opened the wrong box? Children can be a lot like that. Some parents have even gone back to the hospital and checked medical records just to make sure they have the right child because things were not turning out the way they had envisioned.

Child-rearing is not easy. Next to building a good marriage, rearing a child is the hardest task man will ever endeavor. Sadly, the task becomes more difficult every day because our society has become so morally corrupt it seemingly has thrown away all the valued character qualities that God exemplifies for mankind. One wonders what kind of future a child has in such a wicked world.

This certainly reveals to parents the importance of rearing godly children and in doing so can change the course of our future. So if our future's well-being lies in how effective we are in our child-rearing, perhaps we should look at our own methods and standards as parents.

Psalm 127:4 says children are like arrows in the hands of warriors. It would be interesting to find out if children today view their parents as warriors. Are parents today the spiritual warriors that children look up to as steadfast, strong and never wavering in time of battle? Can they trust their parents' aim and will they (the child and the arrow) be released on target? Suppose the arrows (or the child) have imperfections or need fine tuning? What if they keep flying off the target, missing the mark? Will the warrior abandon or give up on them as hopeless or useless, not worth saving?

A study in history will reveal that true warriors during the Old Testament period crafted their own arrows and it cost a great investment of time and patience to complete this task. As they worked on the arrow, they periodically tested it to see if it would fly true. If it did not, the arrow was retrieved regardless of how far off the target it flew. And then more time was spent working on the arrow until it did fly true. The warrior was willing to spend much time with the arrow because his life and future depended upon it in battle.

Like the warrior, parents should be willing to spend much time and energy with their children. It has been estimated that fathers today spend two minutes of time a day with their children, one on one. Is it any wonder that children become rebellious and get into trouble? The modern day warrior is so busy he does not have time to shape his arrows. And to enlist children in programs and sports activities certainly has its value but it should not replace one on one time together. The practice of the true warrior and his arrows was certainly time spent alone, just him and his arrows…shaping, rubbing, fitting, sharpening, testing and retrieving.

Children are a gift from God and He wishes to fill our quivers with them. We need to understand that the world is a battlefield and to rear children so that they develop the victory strength that God intended----we parents must be warriors. Spiritually, parents must be ready to fight the battles necessary to train children and direct them. In doing so, we could be one generation away from changing the course of the world. What a great investment in our future good parenting can be.

RICH MAN, POOR MAN, INDIAN CHIEF

Mike and I have one son, Kelly. We could not have handled two or three boys as some of our friends had. Kelly was all boy as they say, and his personality lay somewhere between Opie Taylor, Dennis the Menace and The Terminator.

As a child Kelly was a very ambitious little fellow, always planning for what he wanted to become when he grew up. It is wonderful for a son to be so ambitious, but there was one problem…Kelly not only planned what he wanted to become when he grew up but he acted out his choices as well. He had a long list of professional aspirations and the list grew daily. He wanted to be a brain surgeon on day, an explosive expert the next and a skydiver the next day. It does not stretch the imagination very far to understand that we spent a number of anxious moments around our household and in the emergency room at the hospital as well.

One hot day in July, he came into the house sweaty and dirty and his clothing was encrusted in leaves, grass and mud from playing in the woods. I was sitting on my beautiful sofa that had just been newly upholstered in the latest Waverly pattern. It was gorgeous and I was so glad to be rid of the old dirty covering that the children had abused for the past years. Most women only get a new sofa four or five times in a lifetime and I had pretty much used up my allotment.

Kelly walked across the room toward me, leaving muddy footprints behind him. There was a deep frown on his ten year old forehead. In his play world he had been working hard at preparing for his future and he obviously had something important on his mind.

He threw himself down beside me as dirt and mud fell onto my beautiful sofa, then he turned two big brown eyes up at me and in an exhausted, whiny voice said, "Mom when I grow up what do you want me to be? In an exasperated, motherly voice I replied, "Twenty-one son, twenty-one".

Jesus said to them, "With men this is impossible, but with God all things are possible." Matthew 19:26

One of the beautiful things about a child is that in their innocent and inexperienced lives they do not place limitations on themselves. At young ages they look at exciting adult careers, events, challenges and decide they can do it too. "I want to be a fireman, an astronaut, a brain surgeon, a house wife, a carpenter, a pro athlete, the president!" and on and on they say. As they look toward the future and daydream they feel that all things are possible.

The adult on the other hand, has learned that failure is a very real possibility in some or many of the things that they may attempt to accomplish. Unfortunately if failure occurs too often there is a tendency to see goals in life as unattainable and give up completely.

God has a powerful perspective on success and attaining the impossible. He looks at each person individually because He created each man and woman uniquely. He looks beyond our human weakness and limitations that we tend to focus on and He focuses on what we can become through Him. God sees in us undeveloped spiritual gifts, talents and potential beyond our wildest dreams. He sees all of these abilities because He has placed them in us. Too often we do not step into uncomfortable territory to develop these abilities because it stretches us and stretching is painful.

There is a story in the Bible about a frightened, weak man who is a perfect example of this dilemma. Gideon worked in a deep wine press beating out wheat. (Judges 6:11) Why was he beating out wheat in a place designed to make wine? Because he was scared to death and the safest place to hide from the evil Midianites who had taunted Israel for years was in the wine press. The Scripture tells us that even though Gideon was a poor prospect for a brave warrior, God sent an angel to speak to him and his opening greeting to Gideon was, "The Lord is with you O valiant warrior." God needed a warrior to rescue His people and he saw a valiant warrior in Gideon. Gideon's response was pretty much, "Who Me?" because he had never experienced brave, leadership abilities within himself. But with God all things are possible so Gideon stepped out into unfamiliar, uncomfortable, stretching territory and became the leader that God desired.

By trusting God and allowing our will to become His will, His goals to become our goals, like Gideon, we can experience success beyond our wildest imagination. Trusting God gives us the courage to reach for dreams beyond our abilities rather than settling for lethargic, lackluster, safe ground.

John Haggai said this beautifully when he said, "Begin something today so impossible that unless God is in it, it is doomed to failure." God does not want us to fail when we are walking out His plan and stretching the abilities within us to do something that is beyond ourselves and appears impossible. He wants others around us to see that with God all things are possible, where we are weak, He is strong.

Paul encouraged young Timothy (who desired to develop God's potential in his life) "Fight the good fight of faith; take hold of the eternal life to which you were called..." (1Timothy 6:12)

Are you ready to "take hold" and live today as if it counts for eternity? Because actually it should---God placed in each of His children abilities and gifts that can impact eternity every day. Our eternity can begin today if we ask God to show up and show out in us!

DAY 27

PEANUT BUTTER PHILOSOPHY

It's strange why homeowners make the statement, "We are really enjoying living in our home!" When actually, with all the work a house demands the statement is not always true. In fact, the opposite is often the case. I often hear myself saying, "I'm dying to get this house painted". And I keep hearing Mike say, "Finishing this basement is killing me." This certainly does not sound like enjoyable living to me. It sounds more like suicide.

This was pretty much our attitude when we were completing the basement in our last home. We were doing much of the work ourselves and many days I would work alone while the family was away at work and school.

On a cold February day I was completing a closet in a bedroom located at the foot of the basement stairs beneath the kitchen. I was rushing to hang a prehung door to the closet before it became too dark and cold to work because the electrical wiring and heating had not yet been completed in this area.

I was inside the closet hanging the door, which is relatively simple to do. Relatively simple if you have a mole's intelligence to take the staves out of the door before you nail the door facing to the two-by-four framing. The staves are small metal spikes driven through the door facing into the door itself to hold the door in place until you are ready to hang it.

I nailed the door to the frame like a professional carpenter. In fact, I put in three times the number of nails needed because I knew our son, Kelly, would eventually use this bedroom when he grew older. Believe me, this door would need all the support it could get.

In the dim battery-lit light inside the closet (that was running out of battery), I stood back and admired my work before pushing at the door to open it. And the moment I pushed the door and it did not budge, I knew I was captured.

Fear, panic, humiliation and sick whimpering are a few emotions that pass through the brain at a time like this. Two minutes earlier I was a proud craftsman, now I was that stupid mole, trapped in a cold dark hole. And because the closet was now dark, I could not see to pull the nails out to free myself.

Unless I tried to kick out the door or the drywall, there was nothing left for me to do but sit on the cold concrete floor and wait until the children came home from school. It did not help my attitude to think about the hot cup of coffee and Snickers bar that I had waiting just outside the door to enjoy after I finished the work.

After what seemed an eternity, the children arrived home from school. My teenage daughter, Paige, responded to my call for help and ran down the stairs to see what was wrong. Angie, who was six, followed her sister down the stairs to see what a mother nailed in a closet looked like. Kelly, who was ten, was unimpressed with my plight and busied himself making his usual peanut butter and jelly sandwich in the kitchen above my closet. I could hear him above me gathering all the necessary items to make his snack. I heard the refrigerator and pantry doors open and close and the silverware rattle as he fumbled for a knife.

Yelling through the closet door, I told Paige how she could help me and she rushed back up the stairs, two at a time. She landed in the kitchen screaming, "Kelly, how can you eat when Mom is trapped and needs our help?"

Licking the last of the jelly from the knife before jamming it into the peanut butter jar up to the handle, Kelly replied, "There's no need to hurry; she's not going anywhere".

"And you shall know the truth and the truth shall set you free". John 8:32

A very comical scene is the picture of a curious raccoon that is given a small-mouth jug with a piece of candy in the bottom. The raccoon pushes his paw into the jug and grabs the candy, but to his dismay finds he cannot take his paw out of the jug. Obviously, with his fist clutched tightly around the candy his paw is too large to slide out. Not willing to give up his treasure, his paw remains trapped in the jug and wearing a jug on his front paw is definitely a handicap to the raccoon's lifestyle.

Can the sinful person identify with this picture? Sadly so! If we are not careful we tend to wrap our lives around so many things on earth that are very important to us and we hang on with a tight grip. Not that all the things on earth are evil in themselves, but if we are not careful they become more important than loving and worshiping our heavenly Father. The scripture will show us that this may result in worshiping the creation more than the Creator which is sin and is a trap which keeps us from developing a close relationship with Jesus Christ.

How are we freed from this trap? The scripture again tells us to admit our sin, whatever it looks like, ask for forgiveness and turn away from it. 1John 1: 9 says "If we confess our sins, He is faithful and righteous to forgive us our sins and to cleanse us from all unrighteousness." Jesus died on the cross to make this verse possible for us. The verse says Jesus not only forgives us but also cleanses us from ALL unrighteousness. This means that when we ask for forgiveness and let go of the grip on the sinful things of the world more important to us than God, then there is nothing in our past lives that can keep God from our present or our future. By the blood of Jesus we are declared clean and righteous.

Satan would like to keep us in the trap by keeping the truth from us, but when we learn the truth and act on it... we are free. Jesus said in John 8:32 "and you shall know the truth and the truth shall make you free." Let's desire to live righteous lives and take our fist out of the jar of deception and live with an open palm to receive Truth.

GRANDMOTHER, WHAT RED EYES YOU HAVE!

Becoming a grandmother was one of those delightful experiences that came into my life and completely surprised me like an unexpected gift of precious value.

Despite the silly description that a grandmother is someone who takes her teeth out at night and wears funny underwear, I looked forward to filling this role in my life with great expectancy.

Soon after our first grandchild's birth on Thanksgiving Day, the main order of business was what she would call me. I supposed she was going to roll over in her tiny bed at any moment and look directly at me and ask, "Who are you?" I had never been a grandmother so I did not know who I was either. How one is addressed is an important decision so I began to put thought to it.

Mike's name as a grandparent was easy---he would be called "Pop." He also decided I would be called "Big Momma." I reminded him that his shirts came in tent size but mine were a size ten and that I would be called "Grandmother Martha."

This was eventually shortened to "Grand Martha" by the grandchildren and sounds as if I am a grand potentate of a Harley bikers association, but it works.

I was able to experience the full joy of grandparenthood when this first grandchild, Jessica, came from Texas to Georgia to spend three weeks with us in December.

Jessica was three at the time and very petite with beautiful long blond hair, brown eyes, and eyelashes that looked like Bambi. Our favorite game was sitting in front of a mirror putting on make-up, tons of jewelry and gasping in long southern drawls, "Oh, you are sooo beautiful (bootiful to a three year old)!" Then we would have a tea party and sip from tiny cups with our pinkies held just right.

Jessica had been with us only two weeks when both of us became ill with a flu that was sweeping the country. To say we were sick was an understatement. Our eyes were red and swollen, our noses were red and swollen, our throats were red and swollen and pain inched its way into every part of our bodies. While I was at my lowest ebb, I overheard the news reporting on T. V. that globally 3,000 people had died with this flu. I was sure none of them had been as sick as I was at that moment.

On the fifth day of the misery, Jessica and I were lying in bed together trying to sleep as much as possible. It was during one of my semi-conscious states that I realized someone was staring at me. I slowly opened narrow slits on my face where my eyes usually were to find Jessica lying with her head on my pillow a few inches from my face. She was sucking her thumb and watching me closely through a thicket of tangled blond hair. After several moments of complete silence and unblinking eye-to-eye contact, Jessica slowly pulled her thumb from her mouth and whispered hoarsely, "Grand Martha, you're not bootiful anymore."

I was sure I was not...but most of me was alive.

"Strength and dignity are her clothing and
she smiles at the future." Proverbs 31:25

Our society today is caught up with a tremendous priority placed on surface beauty. Men, women and children spend one-third of their time and energy preparing their wardrobes, hair and make-up and three thirds of their income paying for it all.

It should be no surprise that this trend is true when television, magazines, newspaper and internet advertising emphasizes physical beauty as the most important focus in life.

There are no boundaries on the ages of those who are pressured by the importance of surface beauty. The elderly buy creams and undergo cosmetic surgery while young mothers buy expensive designer tennis shoes for their infants who will outgrow them by dark. Women from teens to middle age dress their bodies in nudity and sensuality not understanding that their bodies are a private garden not the public park.

The victorious woman in Proverbs 31 speaks of being well-dressed and beautiful for her husband which is most important for a wife. But she also is aware her real beauty comes from within and this is where she places her priority. "Strength and dignity are her clothing" she proclaims. Her strength comes from God and dignity comes from obedience to His Word.

Isaiah 61:3 tells us, "...a planting of the Lord for the display of My Splendor."

She is able to smile in confidence at the future rather than being anxious because growing older may leave her unattractive and unproductive to society.

> The scripture says, "Planted in the house of the Lord,
> They will flourish in the courts of our God.
> They will still yield fruit in old age;
> They shall be full of sap and very green,
> To declare that the Lord is upright;
> He is my rock and there is no
> unrighteousness in Him."
> Psalm 92:13-15

A woman's true beauty is within and even though the years may wear on her body, her beauty in the Lord grows more beautiful as she clothes herself in His righteousness and glory.

I realize this may sound unattractive to the world but I am going to work on being "full of sap and very green". It keeps us young!

TEENAGE TERRITORIAL TURF

Teenagers and clean bedrooms have always been on opposite ends of the pole, or at least that was true with all three of our children. Being a boy or girl had nothing to do with the problem, being a teenager was the common denominator.

Our third child, Angie, seemed to be typical of this adolescent disorder and her bedroom always looked like a waste land. I had read where waste lands bred disease and death so I avoided her room as much as possible.

Not only did her room drive us crazy because of the mess, but we often had guests in our home and I could not bear the thought of someone seeing this disgraceful scene. Angie's theory was---she knew where everything was, she liked it that way, and no one would see it but her. Her pledge to me was that when we had guests in our home to simply tell her and she would clean it up...maybe. Meanwhile, I hoped the health department did not confuse her room as an annex to the city dump.

We continued to live with this agreement between us until one day I returned home from shopping and disturbed an intruder in our house. I was not sure if he was still in the house or if he had completed his mischief and left, so I frantically called the police and waited on the street for their arrival.

Of course when the police arrived they had to very methodically examine each room in search of the thief and report any damage or loss that may have occured. Room by room they searched through the house. They examined behind every closed door and they allowed me to follow behind at a safe distance to point out possible hiding places.

Eventually they came to Angie's room. A young officer threw open the door and quickly pointed his revolver into the room. His eyes grew large and his jaw line tightened as his eyes and revolver moved slowly around the room. I slowly moved up behind him and looked over his shoulder and the scene was frightening. There was clothing on the floor and hanging on the bed post. The dresser drawers were all open with clothing spilling out onto the floor. The closet looked as if a volcano had erupted and clothing was oozing out onto the floor like molted lava. Books, papers and half eaten snacks lay over the unmade bed. Pom-poms and sports paraphernalia completely covered a chair and every shoe she owned was piled in the middle of the floor.

The officer yelled back over his shoulder to another officer down the hall, "Sam, they have really plundered this room. It's a wreck." Then he glanced back at me and said, "Better stand back ma'am, it's not safe to come in here yet".

Looking over the officer's shoulder into the room I saw it was just as Angie had left it that morning. I audaciously agreed with the officer and replied "Your right officer, it's not safe to go in there yet."

> *For you, yourselves know full well that the day of*
> *the Lord will come like a thief in the night.*
> *1 Thessalonians 5:2*

Just as our daughter Angie had planned to be prepared by an advance warning when guests arrived in our home, many people today plan to prepare for the coming of Jesus Christ by an advance warning as well. They live under the assumption that there will always be tomorrow and plenty of time to do what is necessary even at the last minute.

However, God's Word has been giving the advance warning for more than two thousand years and it tells us we only have today, this moment even, because we do not know what life will be like tomorrow. (James 4:14) Jesus' coming can be "like a thief in the night". But our loving God gave clear instructions about how to make preparation:

We first acknowledge in our head and heart that God loved us so much that He sent His only Son, Jesus, to do what we cannot do; be the perfect sacrifice for our sins (John 3:16). We must also acknowledge that despite His death on the cross, Jesus is a living God. 1Corinthians 15:4 explains that Jesus was buried and that He arose from the grave on the third day according to the scriptures.

Secondly we must do extensive housecleaning in our heart. There is sin there and it must be confessed as the scripture in 1 John 1:9 says, "If we confess our sins, He is faithful and righteous to forgive us our sins and to cleanse us from all unrighteousness." So we must confess that sin is disobedience to God's Word and allow our hearts to be truly remorseful and ask Jesus to forgive us of our sins.

And third, now is the time to pray a simple prayer of faith accepting Jesus Christ as your Lord and Savior. Understanding who Jesus is and that He is a gift of God is not the same as accepting the gift. That is why praying a prayer of acceptance is important for us if we are to be prepared for His coming. Pray this simple pray aloud or silently, but pause and be intentional in saying the most important words you will ever speak.

"Father, I know that your son, Jesus, sacrificed his life on a cross for my sins so that I may receive forgiveness and have eternal life in heaven. I believe that Jesus was buried but arose from the grave on the third day and is a living God. I understand that I have sinned and I confess these acts of sin and ask for forgiveness and am truly sorry for sins I have committed against you. And now Jesus, I accept you as my Lord and Savior. In Jesus name, Amen."

Having just made the most important decision of your life you are about to take an extraordinary journey through life. Jesus has well-equipped you to take this journey by placing within you the Helper, the Holy Spirit.

Jesus said in Acts 1:8, "but you shall receive power when the Holy Spirit has come upon you." This is power to live the Christian life God desires for us to live here on earth. It is the power to overcome Satan and face the trials and tribulations victoriously that come into our lives. Jesus gave His followers all power and authority over all the demons, and to heal diseases (see Luke 1:9). We must instinctively draw upon the power of the Holy Spirit within us to live this life promised to us.

And most importantly it is power to complete the work God has planned for us to do for Him here on earth. The Bible says in

1 Corinthians 12:7, "Each person is given something to do that shows who God is: Everyone gets in on it, everyone benefits". (The Message Bible) When we find this place in life, we are ready for His coming.

DAY 30

WAR WOMAN

It is amazing how a family begins as a young husband and wife with all of life before them and at that point in life everything seems possible. And when there is only the two of them the world revolves around them and their plans for the future. Then the family is defined by the number of children they usher into the world, and in mine and Mike's case we were defined as five after adding three children. Years sped by like a runaway freight train and eight grandchildren were added and the once young family of two now numbers thirteen. But procreation does not stop there; the great-grandchildren begin and the total number escalates as the years accumulate. And we count it all joy.

Mike and I both have Native American ancestry and have always looked back at great- great-grandparents roots with pride. We want our grandchildren to know their ancestral roots as well so we have watched their personalities and given each child a pet name that reflects his or her Native American heritage.

Our oldest grandchild, Jessica, as a young child was very petite and blond, but she could act like a tribe of Indians on a war path if upset---so we called her Jessawah.

Our first born grandson, Michael, for some unknown reason had a fixation on his pointer finger and how many holes he could punch into any surface he encountered. His little finger was always poking a hole in whatever was around him. And if he could not do it by himself, with drooling lips around his pacifier, he cried out to his mother…"Poke a hole Mamma!" So his name came easy---Chief Poke-a-Hole.

Our second-born grandson, Gavin, was always into everything around him---nothing was safe. If he was loose in the house all you had to do was wait for the crash because sooner or later something was going to be pulled down from above him and a crash followed. I called him---Thunder Boy.

Second-born granddaughter, Erin, was born a baby squaw with her loud crying and big voice. She had a strong will and was stubborn as a post so we called her---Girl Who Stands With Tight Fist.

Third-born granddaughter, Jordan, was sweet and docile as could be unless we would not give her what she wanted and then watch out! She always had a pacifier in her mouth and if you threatened her in any way she would pull the pacifier from her drooling mouth and throw it at you like a spear and put it right on the mark. She earned the title---Girl with Wet Arrow.

Fourth-born granddaughter, Carly, came into the world laughing, melancholy and happy- go-lucky. She was always having such a good time in life she only half listened to what was being said to her. Information just went in one ear and out the other. We call her---Tell Her Two Times, because you had to…every time.

Our third grandson, Taylor, was never still, he was always busy and he ran everywhere he went. He also talked so fast he could have been speaking Cherokee for all we know because we never understood what he was saying. I took a while to name him but came up with ---Talking Boy With Fast Feet.

The fourth and last grandson, Beau, came along later after the first seven, so he was the family's new baby after not having one for so long. I called him Beau Baby until he was too old to be called a baby's name. But after watching his melancholy mood swings, his tender heart and faith in God, I called him---Boy Who Makes Peace.

On a summer day when the first seven grandchildren were small they were all at "Grand Martha's house" and I played the role of baby sitter. We were all out in the yard playing and one of them ran up to me and asked if they could all play on the tennis court. I said sure, as long as they did not take their bikes, tricycles, and skateboards onto the court. The wheels would cut up the surface of the court. "Oh no, Grand Martha we would never do that," they chimed out innocently. I left them to play while I ran in the house to fix a quick lunch.

I shortly returned outside and when I walked near the tennis court it looked like the state park. The children all had their bicycles, tricycles, skate boards, skates and anything with wheels, riding wildly on my court. I stomped onto the court and let them have it verbally and told them how disobedient they had been. Then I told them to get their wheels off the court and go inside and wash their hands and get ready for lunch.

Back in the kitchen they all sat quietly around the table while I served them. Eventually, Girl Who Stands With Tight Fist, who had previously been appointed as spokesman, spoke up timidly, "Grand Martha, do you know your Indian name?" I swung my head around to a full eye to eye stare at the spokesman and replied with raised eyebrows, "No," I said crisply, "what is it?" All of the tribe war whooped together and cried, "War Woman!"

I knew they had hit bulls-eye and I was ready to scalp them all---then smooch kisses all over their sweet cheeks.

> **"You are our letter written in our hearts, known and read by men." 2 Corinthians 3:2 & 3**

The apostle Paul was writing to the new Christians in the church in Corinth commending them on the obedient manner in which they were living out his teachings of God's Word. Paul lovingly writes that their lives were a letter written on his heart because they were glorifying God so beautifully. And not only was his heart touched, but the hearts of people observing the lives of the Corinthian Christians were touched as well. They saw changed lives as a result of the Christ-centered teachings of Paul.

There is no higher compliment to a teacher than seeing these positive results...students living successfully despite inexperience and challenging trials. The students' victorious lives became a letter, not written on a tablet of stone, but on each of their hearts' and on Paul's heart as well.

I believe this can also be a picture of godly parents and grandparents who pour Christ's teaching into their children and grandchildren. And when our offspring "eventually" learn these truths, (they can be stubborn!) others' watching will see that God's principles are a worthy choice as a lifestyle. Then ultimately, God is glorified and the family is strengthened in the present generation and in future generations as well. So like Paul, our children and grandchildren become a precious letter written on the hearts of parents and grandparents.

What a legacy for parents and grandparents to leave on earth, more valuable than an inheritance of silver and gold. Most parents work hard their entire lives to leave their off- spring things money can buy---stuff---and more stuff---when the child's most precious inheritance is found in learning godly character and the principles of God's Word.

God's Word says, "My people perish for lack of knowledge," and sadly many of our children have and will perish spiritually, emotionally, and physically because they are not taught the Word of God as a standard for a successful life. Statistics reveal today that many of our younger generation's lives reveal lack of courage, careless decisions and moral compromise. Could this survey be a result of the fact that the majority of our younger generations have never seen the miraculous power of God? Perhaps this is true because they have never seen miracles in their parent's or grandparent's lives. Nor have they been told that miracles exist for today.

Without believing the miraculous power of God, we rear a generation of children who never experience God's potential and purpose in their lives. They give up and loose hope before the gifts within them are developed and God's promised blessing manifest. They do not know that in our life journey in order to accomplish God ordained destiny, it will require God powered miracles to develop potential, purpose and promised blessings.

So let's read on! Verse 3 follows and tells us that if our children and grandchildren are taught God's Word, this is what we can expect… "*being manifested that you are a letter of Christ, cared for by us, written not with ink, but with the Spirit of the living God, not on tablets of stone, but on tablets of human hearts.*" This wonderful verse tells us:

- ✓ Our offspring will live out the teachings of Christ with gusto (manifested power) if we nurture and teach them.
- ✓ Our children will be a letter of Christ and for many people our children's lives may be the only letter (Bible) they see.
- ✓ Because of what Jesus did on the cross, God's law is no longer written on stone tablets nor with ink, but upon our children's hearts through the Holy Spirit resulting in a personal relationship with God himself.

The short version:

The world will see our children's and grandchildren's love and obedience for Christ as they live it out loud each day. The Amplified Bible says it beautifully in verse 2 "…*you yourselves are our letter of recommendation (our credentials) written in your hearts, to be known (recognized) and read by everybody*". What a legacy to leave, there is none greater.

POST SCRIPT

I pray this book will be written words of legacy from me and Mike to our children and grandchildren. True to life in a fallen world, our journey has experienced set-backs, heartbreaks and disappointments. But by the faithfulness of God, there have been many more victories and miracles along our highway of life than disappointments. As I close this book we have recently been blessed to see the results of our prayers and diligent work of raising a family.

We have the blessing of our first two great-grandchild, born to
Thunder Boy and wife Michelle.
Great-grandson's name...Gideon, Mighty Warrior!
Second great-grandchild born to
Jessawah and husband Stephen.
Great-grandson's name...Jude, Praise!

Printed in the United States
By Bookmasters

Printed in the United States
By Bookmasters